Great Escapes
Mediterranean

Edited & compiled by Angelika Taschen *Texts by* Christiane Reiter

Great Escapes
Mediterranean

TASCHEN

HONG KONG KÖLN LONDON LOS ANGELES MADRID PARIS TOKYO

Contents   Inhalt   Sommaire

Price categories:		Preiskategorien:		Catégories de prix:	
€	up to 150 €	€	bis 150 €	€	jusqu'à 150 €
€€	up to 250 €	€€	bis 250 €	€€	jusqu'à 250 €
€€€	up to 450 €	€€€	bis 450 €	€€€	jusqu'à 450 €
€€€€	over 450 €	€€€€	über 450 €	€€€€	plus de 450 €

"Life without celebrations is a long road without inns."
Democritus (c. 460 – c. 370 BCE)

ENGLAND

NETHER-
LAN...

BELGIUM

FRANCE

PORTUGAL

SPAIN

MOROCCO

ALGERIA

A Sojourn in Utopia

Hôtel Le Corbusier, Marseille

Hôtel Le Corbusier, Marseille

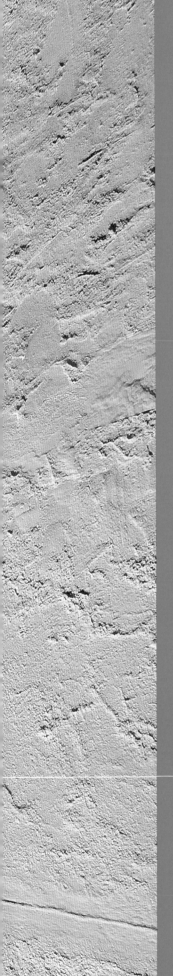

A Sojourn in Utopia

"La maison du fada", the house of the crazy – that was the nickname the Marseillais gave Le Corbusier's "Cité Radieuse" when it was completed in 1952. The idea behind the apartment block, which towers imposingly on mighty concrete pillars and is reminiscent of a steamer in dry dock, appeared dubious to them – but Le Corbusier wanted to solve the housing shortage problem after the Second World War by means of utopian town planning. He constructed a "vertical city" within a city – with individual residential units and hallways that led like streets through the buildings, as well as shops and even schools, all strictly designed according to his theories of proportions and chromatics. Though for many his concept never completely came off, the "Cité Radieuse", still inhabited and today under a preservation order, is a key piece of modern architecture and a pilgrimage site for admirers of Le Corbusier. They can stay overnight here in authentic style: the Hotel Le Corbusier on the third and fourth floors occupies former apartments, designed true to the original. Guests can experience this architectural heritage in all its purity in the 170-square-foot cabins, which recall the cells in the La Tourette monastery, also designed by Le Corbusier, and are fitted out with furnishings by Charlotte Perriand. But those wishing for more room (and a view across Marseilles all the way to the sea) will also discover reminiscences in the studios and rooms, such as Le Corbusier's chaise longue or original kitchens. These features are, however, no longer in working order, serving these days only as stylish decoration.

Books to pack: "The Radiant City" by Le Corbusier and "The Marseilles Trilogy" by Jean-Claude Izzo.

Hôtel Le Corbusier	
280 Boulevard Michelet	
13008 Marseille	
France	
Tel. +33 4 9116 7800	
Fax +33 4 9116 7828	
contact@hotellecorbusier.com	
www.hotellecorbusier.com	
Open all year round	

DIRECTIONS	In a park in the east of Marseilles; just over a mile from the sea, 19 miles from the airport.
RATES	€
ROOMS	21 rooms.
FOOD	"Le Ventre de l'Architecte" serves simple French meals.
HISTORY	The "Cité Radieuse" is one of five "Unités d'Habitations" built by Le Corbusier in France and Berlin. The hotel in its current form was opened by Alban and Dominique Gérardin in 2003.
X-FACTOR	Just as Le Corbusier intended, guests are permitted use of the rooftop pool and all leisure facilities in the "city within a city".

Wohnen in Utopia

»La maison du fada«, das Haus des Verrückten – so nannten
die Marseiller Le Corbusiers »Cité Radieuse«, als sie 1952
fertiggestellt war. Die Idee hinter dem Block, der auf mäch-
tigen Betonstelzen thront und an einen Dampfer im
Trockendock erinnert, schien ihnen nicht geheuer – wollte
Le Corbusier das Wohnungsbauproblem nach dem Zweiten
Weltkrieg doch mittels einer Utopie der Stadtplanung lösen.
Er konstruierte eine »vertikale Stadt« in der Stadt – mit
streng nach seiner Proportions- und Farbenlehre entworfenen Wohneinheiten, Fluren, die wie Straßen durchs Gebäude
führen, Geschäften und sogar Schulen. Sein Konzept mag für
viele niemals ganz aufgegangen sein, doch die immer noch
bewohnte und heute denkmalgeschützte »Cité Radieuse«
ist ein Schlüsselbauwerk moderner Architektur und eine
Pilgerstätte für Le-Corbusier-Anhänger. Diese können hier
stilecht übernachten: In ehemaligen Apartments im dritten
und vierten Stock ist das Hotel Le Corbusier untergebracht
und originalgetreu gestaltet. Ganz pur erlebt man das archi-
tektonische Erbe in den nur 16 Quadratmeter umfassenden
Kabinen, die an die Zellen des von Le Corbusier entworfenen
Klosters La Tourette erinnern und mit Mobiliar von Charlotte
Perriand eingerichtet sind. Wer mehr Platz (und Blick über
Marseille bis zum Meer!) wünscht, entdeckt aber auch in den
Studios und Zimmern Reminiszenzen – etwa Le Corbusiers
Chaiselongue oder Originalküchen. Diese sind allerdings
nicht mehr funktionsfähig, sondern nur noch stilvolle
Dekoration.
**Buchtipps: »Städtebau« von Le Corbusier und
»Die Marseille-Trilogie« von Jean-Claude Izzo.**

Vivre l'utopie

« La maison du fada » – c'est ainsi que les Marseillais ont
surnommé la « Cité Radieuse » de Le Corbusier, une fois
achevée en 1952. L'idée se cachant derrière cet îlot, trônant
sur d'imposants piliers en béton et rappelant un paquebot
à sec, leur semblait plutôt étrange – alors que Le Corbusier
voulait résoudre les problèmes de logement au lendemain de
la Seconde Guerre mondiale grâce à une utopie urbanistique.
Il a construit une « cité-jardin verticale » dans la ville : des
ensembles de logements individuels conçus strictement
d'après ses théories de proportions et de couleurs, des couloirs
qui traversent le bâtiment comme des rues, des magasins
et même des écoles. Son concept n'a probablement pas été
compris par tous mais la « Cité Radieuse », toujours habitée
et classée de nos jours au patrimoine des monuments historiques, est un bâtiment clé de l'architecture moderne et un
lieu de pèlerinage pour les adeptes du Corbusier. L'hôtel Le
Corbusier leur propose une expérience unique : dormir dans
un lieu où rien n'a changé depuis sa création. L'hôtel composé
d'anciens appartements est situé aux troisième et quatrième
étages et reste fidèle à la conception originale. Ces chambres
cabines de seize mètres carrés, qui rappellent les cellules du
monastère de La Tourette créées également par Le Corbusier
et équipées de mobilier dessiné par Charlotte Perriand,
abritent un héritage architectonique à l'état pur. Des studios
et grandes chambres (avec vue sur Marseille et la mer) recèlent
aussi des réminiscences comme la chaise longue de Le
Corbusier ou des cuisines d'origine qui ne sont désormais
que décoratives.
**Livres à emporter : « L'urbanisme » de Le Corbusier et
« La trilogie marseillaise » de Jean-Claude Izzo.**

ANREISE	In einem Park im Osten von Marseille gelegen; 2 km vom Meer, 30 km vom Flughafen entfernt.
PREISE	€
ZIMMER	21 Zimmer.
KÜCHE	»Le Ventre de l'Architecte« serviert einfache französische Menüs.
GESCHICHTE	Die »Cité Radieuse« ist eine von fünf »Unités d'Habita-tions«, die Le Corbusier in Frankreich und Berlin baute. Das Hotel in seiner heutigen Form wurde von Alban und Dominique Gérardin 2003 eröffnet.
X-FAKTOR	Ganz im Sinne Le Corbusiers dürfen Gäste den Dachpool und alle Freizeiteinrichtungen mitbenutzen.

ACCÈS	Dans un parc à l'est de Marseille ; à 2 km de la mer, à 30 km de l'aéroport.
PRIX	€
CHAMBRES	21 chambres.
RESTAURATION	« Le Ventre de l'Architecte » sert une cuisine française de qualité.
HISTOIRE	La « Cité Radieuse » est une des cinq unités d'habita-tions construites en France et à Berlin. L'hôtel a été repris par Alban et Dominique Gérardin en 2003.
LES « PLUS »	Tout à fait dans l'esprit de Le Corbusier, les clients peuvent profiter de la piscine sur le toit et de toutes les activités proposées dans « la ville dans la ville ».

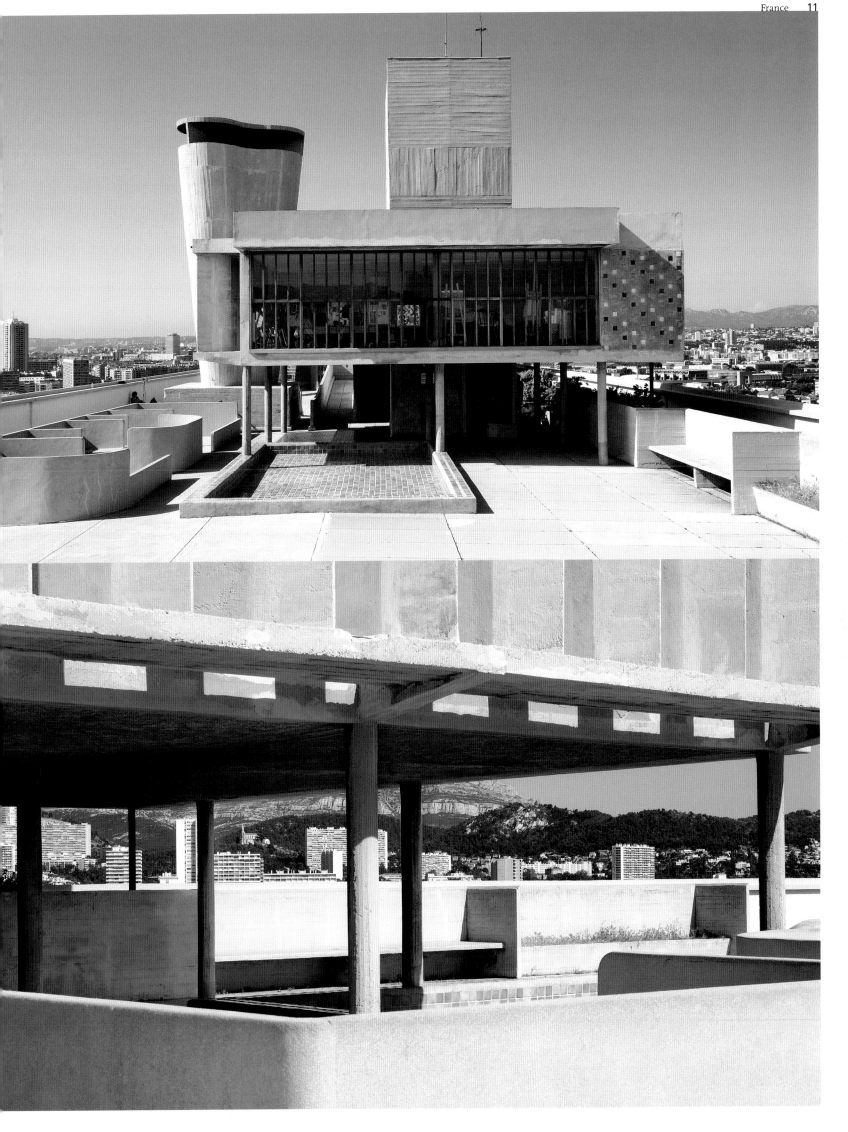

Be King of the Castle
Château de Cassis, Cassis

Château de Cassis, Cassis

Be King of the Castle

Once this castle above the limestone cliffs of Cassis belonged to the imperium of the Les Baux family – the legendary dynasty that, at its peak, exercised its mighty rule over almost 80 towns and villages in the region and had the castle converted into a fortress housing 250 residents. It is difficult to imagine so many people up here today: with just nine rooms, Château de Cassis is one of the most exclusive "chambres d'hôtes" in Provence – a guest house that eschews official hotel status and an endless list of services, instead offering an uncomplicated ambience and an individual design. During years of renovation work the young owner Chloé Caussin has, in all the right places, either erased or emphasised the marks left by history, and under the old vaulting mixes styles in a carefree manner: so it is that the "Suite Romantique" is fitted out with classic furniture and maintained in pastel shades (it even has its own small piano for any descendants of minnesingers), in the "La Tour" suite futuristic bedside tables, made of metal, will take guests by surprise, and the "Suite Marocaine" exudes Middle Eastern charm thanks to its warm colours, a four-poster bed and Moroccan accessories. Not all the rooms have a sea view – those wishing to enjoy the panorama in absolute privacy are best served by the "La Jean Baptiste" suite with its lovely veranda. But on the communal terraces, too, you are unlikely to be disturbed while admiring the bay – after all, the castle luckily has only nine rooms.

Book to pack: "My Father's Glory & My Mother's Castle" by Marcel Pagnol.

Château de Cassis	
Traverse du Château	
13260 Cassis	
France	
Tel. +33 4 4201 6320	
Fax +33 4 4201 7358	
chateaudecassis@free.fr	
www.chateaudecassis.com	
Open all year round	

DIRECTIONS	On the coast between Marseilles and Toulon, 34 miles from Marseilles Airport.
RATES	€€
ROOMS	3 rooms, 6 suites.
FOOD	Normally only French breakfast is served; however dinner can be arranged on request.
HISTORY	In Roman antiquity there was a watchtower here, from which the "Castrum Carcisis" developed. After the Les Baux era the castle fell into disrepair until it was opened as a guest house in 2005.
X-FACTOR	The pool in the middle of the walled garden.

Heute ein Burgherr

Einst gehörte dieses Schloss über der Kalksteinküste von Cassis zum Imperium der Familie Les Baux – der legendären Dynastie, die auf dem Höhepunkt ihrer Macht über fast 80 Orte der Region herrschte und die Burg zu einer Festung für 250 Bewohner ausbauen ließ. So viele Menschen kann man sich hier oben heute kaum mehr vorstellen: Mit gerade einmal neun Zimmern ist das Château de Cassis eines der exklusivsten »Chambres d'Hôtes« der Provence – ein Gästehaus, das auf offiziellen Hotelstatus sowie eine Endlosliste von Services verzichtet und stattdessen unkompliziertes Ambiente sowie individuelles Design bietet. Die junge Besitzerin Chloé Caussin hat in jahrelanger Renovierungsarbeit die Spuren der Geschichte an den jeweils richtigen Stellen getilgt oder betont und mischt unter alten Gewölben unbeschwert die Stile: So ist die »Suite Romantique« mit klassischen Möbeln ausgestattet und in Pastell gehalten (sie besitzt für Nachfahren der Minnesänger sogar ein eigenes Klavier), in der Suite »La Tour« überraschen futuristische Nachtschränkchen aus Metall, und die »Suite Marocaine« verströmt dank warmer Farben, eines Himmelbetts und marokkanischer Accessoires orientalisches Flair. Nicht alle Räume eröffnen Meerblick – wer das Panorama ganz privat genießen möchte, ist mit der Suite »La Jean Baptiste« mit schöner Veranda am besten bedient. Aber auch auf den öffentlichen Terrassen wird man beim Bewundern der Bucht von Cassis kaum gestört – das Schloss besitzt ja glücklicherweise nur neun Zimmer.

Buchtipp: »Das Schloss meiner Mutter« von Marcel Pagnol.

Châtelain d'un jour

Trônant majestueusement au-dessus des falaises de calcaire de Cassis, ce château faisait partie autrefois de l'empire de la famille des Baux, une dynastie légendaire, qui au plus fort de son pouvoir régna sur plus de 80 villages de la région et fit transformer le château en une forteresse accueillant 250 habitants. De nos jours, il est difficile d'imaginer autant de monde là-haut : avec ses neuf chambres, le château de Cassis est une des « chambres d'hôtes » les plus luxueuses de Provence. Il renonce au statut officiel d'hôtel ainsi qu'à une liste infinie de prestations et propose à la place une ambiance détendue et un design individuel. La jeune propriétaire Chloé Caussin a, durant de longues années de travaux de restauration, effacé ou accentué aux bons endroits les traces de l'histoire. Sous les vieux arcs voûtés, les styles sont mélangés avec audace : la suite romantique aux teintes pastel est aménagée de meubles classiques (elle possède un piano pour les descendants des troubadours), la suite « La Tour » surprend avec ses petites tables de nuit futuristes en métal et des couleurs chaudes, le lit à badaquin et les accessoires marocains confèrent à la suite marocaine un air oriental. Toutes les chambres n'ont pas vue sur la mer. Pour profiter pleinement du panorama, la suite « Jean Baptiste » dotée d'une terrasse privée est la plus belle. Mais il est également possible d'admirer la baie de Cassis en toute tranquillité depuis les terrasses communes – par bonheur, le château n'abrite que neuf chambres.

Livre à emporter : « Le château de ma mère » de Marcel Pagnol.

ANREISE	An der Küste zwischen Marseille und Toulon gelegen, 55 km vom Flughafen Marseille entfernt.
PREISE	€€
ZIMMER	3 Zimmer, 6 Suiten.
KÜCHE	Regulär gibt es nur französisches Frühstück; auf Anfrage können aber Dinner reserviert werden.
GESCHICHTE	In der römischen Antike stand hier ein Wachturm, aus dem sich das »Castrum Carcisis« entwickelte. Nach der Ära Les Baux verfiel das Schloss, bis es 2005 als Gästehaus eröffnet wurde.
X-FAKTOR	Der Pool inmitten des ummauerten Gartens.

ACCÈS	Sur la côte entre Marseille et Toulon, à 55 km de l'aéroport de Marseille.
PRIX	€€
CHAMBRES	3 chambres, 6 suites.
RESTAURATION	Petit déjeuner ; table d'hôtes sur demande.
HISTOIRE	Une tour de guet se dressait ici dans la Rome antique, elle s'est développée ensuite en « Castrum Carcisis ». Après l'extinction de la famille des Baux, le château est tombé en ruine. Les chambres d'hôtes ont ouvert leurs portes en 2005.
LES « PLUS »	La piscine au milieu du jardin, avec vue sur les murs de l'enceinte.

The Flair of the Riviera
Villa Marie, Ramatuelle

Villa Marie, Ramatuelle

The Flair of the Riviera

It was the "Années folles", the crazy years of the French Riviera – the golden age between the First and the Second World War when the Côte d'Azur attracted painters such as Picasso and Matisse and authors like Somerset Maugham, Aldous Huxley and Colette, as well as Europe's high nobility, first and foremost Edward VIII and Wallis Simpson. Its climate and its landscapes, its light and its colours made the Blue Coast a dream destination par excellence. Today the aura of this era has unfortunately disappeared in most places – anyone wishing to experience the region as the artists and bohemians of yesteryear did has to know the area well and include establishments such as the Villa Marie on the travel itinerary. Jocelyne and Jean-Louis Sibuet have designed the property as a tribute to the Côte d'Azur's finest hour. Far removed from the tourist hustle and bustle and situated in a park with palms, pines and cacti, the villa has the appearance of a luxurious private house. The mixture of Baroque armchairs and Provençal wrought-iron furniture, fat-bellied vases and delicate shells, sparkling crystal lights and classic Doric columns sounds bold, but emerges as a total work of art with as much style as charm. No one room is like another – if given the choice, book a sea view and, at least once, dine at a corner table on the terrace: the view across Pampelonne Bay is so fit for the canvas or the page, you'll wish you could paint or write – like the Riviera's famous visitors back in the "Années folles".

Books to pack: "These Pleasures" by Colette and "The Book of the Riviera" by Klaus & Erika Mann.

Villa Marie

Route des Plages – Chemin Val de Rian
83350 Ramatuelle, St Tropez
France
Tel. +33 4 9497 4022
Fax +33 4 9497 3755
contact@villamarie.fr
www.villamarie.fr
**Open from the end of April
to the beginning of October**

DIRECTIONS	Located on a slope in the village of Ramatuelle, west of St Tropez and 62 miles southwest of Nice Airport.
RATES	€€€€
ROOMS	42 rooms.
FOOD	The restaurant serves fine Provençal cuisine; the bar, with a panoramic view, has wines of the region.
HISTORY	The hotel, which includes a lovely spa, was opened in June 2003.
X-FACTOR	Those who don't wish to travel the 4 miles to Pampelonne beach will find a veritable oasis at the organically shaped pool.

Das Flair der Riviera

Es waren die »Années folles«, die verrückten Jahre der Französischen Riviera – die goldenen Zeiten zwischen dem Ersten und Zweiten Weltkrieg, als die Côte d'Azur Maler wie Picasso und Matisse anzog, Schriftsteller wie Somerset Maugham, Aldous Huxley und Colette sowie Europas Hochadel, allen voran Edward VIII. und Wallis Simpson. Ihr Klima und ihre Landschaften, ihr Licht und ihre Farben machten die blaue Küste zum Traumziel par excellence. Heute ist das Flair dieser Epoche leider an den meisten Orten verflogen – wer die Region wie einst die Künstler und Bohemians erleben möchte, muss sich gut auskennen und Adressen wie die Villa Marie auf seine Reiseroute setzen. Jocelyne und Jean-Louis Sibuet haben das Anwesen als Hommage an die schönsten Zeiten der Côte d'Azur gestaltet. Abseits vom Touristentrubel und in einem Park mit Palmen, Pinien und Kakteen gelegen, wirkt die Villa wie ein luxuriöses Privathaus. Die Mischung aus barocken Sesseln und provenzalischen Eisenmöbeln, dickbauchigen Vasen und filigranen Muscheln, funkelnden Kristallleuchtern und klassisch dorischen Säulen klingt mutig – entpuppt sich aber als Gesamtkunstwerk mit ebenso viel Stil wie Charme. Kein Zimmer gleicht dem anderen – wer die Wahl hat, sollte Meerblick buchen sowie mindestens ein Dinner an einem Ecktisch auf der Terrasse: Die Sicht über die Bucht von Pampelonne ist so leinwandtauglich, dass man sich wünscht, malen oder schreiben zu können – wie damals die berühmten Riviera-Besucher der »Années folles«.
Buchtipps: »Die Freuden des Lebens« von Colette und »Das Buch von der Riviera« von Klaus & Erika Mann.

Le charme de la Riviera

C'était les Années folles sur la Riviera française, l'époque bénie entre la Première et la Seconde Guerre mondiale lorsque la Côte d'Azur attirait des peintres comme Picasso et Matisse, des écrivains comme Somerset Maugham, Aldous Huxley et Colette ainsi que la haute noblesse européenne, Edouard VIII et Wallis Simpson ayant ouvert la marche. Son climat et ses paysages, sa lumière et ses couleurs faisaient de la Côte d'Azur une destination de rêve. Malheureusement, le charme de cette époque a disparu en de nombreux endroits. Si vous voulez voir la région comme les artistes et la bohème d'autrefois, vous devez bien connaître la côte et vous rendre à des adresses comme la Villa Marie. Jocelyne et Jean-Louis Sibuet ont aménagé cette propriété en rendant hommage à la Côte d'Azur de l'entre-deux-guerres. A l'écart des touristes, cette villa nichée dans un parc planté de palmiers, de pins et de cactus, a l'air d'une luxueuse demeure privée. Le mélange des fauteuils baroques et des meubles en fer forgé provençaux, des jarres ventrues et des coquillages filigranes, des lustres en cristal étincelants et des colonnes doriques classiques est audacieux, mais crée une œuvre d'art totale harmonieuse et séduisante. Aucune chambre ne ressemble à l'autre. Si vous avez le choix, réservez une chambre avec vue sur la mer et une table en terrasse, au moins un soir et si possible dans un angle : la vue sur la baie de Pampelonne est si pittoresque que l'on aimerait savoir peindre ou écrire, à l'instar des célèbres hôtes séjournant sur la Riviera pendant les Années folles.
Livres à emporter : « La naissance du jour » de Colette et « Le livre sur la Riviera» de Klaus & Erika Mann.

ANREISE	Am Hang im Dorf Ramatuelle gelegen, westlich von St. Tropez und 100 km südwestlich vom Flughafen Nizza.
PREISE	€€€€
ZIMMER	42 Zimmer.
KÜCHE	Das Restaurant serviert feine provenzalische Menüs, die Bar mit Panoramablick Weine der Region.
GESCHICHTE	Das Hotel, zu dem auch ein schönes Spa gehört, wurde im Juni 2003 eröffnet.
X-FAKTOR	Wer nicht bis zum 6 km entfernten Strand von Pampelonne fahren will, findet am organisch geformten Pool eine Oase.

ACCÈS	Sur la colline de Ramatuelle, à l'ouest de Saint-Tropez et à 100 km au sud-ouest de l'aéroport de Nice.
PRIX	€€€€
CHAMBRES	42 chambres.
RESTAURATION	Le restaurant propose des menus provençaux raffinés et le bar avec vue panoramique, des vins de la région.
HISTOIRE	L'hôtel, doté d'un beau spa, a ouvert ses portes en juin 2003.
LES « PLUS »	Si vous ne voulez pas vous rendre à la plage de Pampelonne à 6 km, la piscine de forme organique est une véritable oasis.

Little London in St Tropez
Pastis Hôtel St Tropez, St Tropez

Pastis Hôtel St Tropez, St Tropez

Little London in St Tropez

Ever since the Scottish author Tobias Smollett published his travel letters from southern Europe in the mid-18th century, penning line after line of praise for the French coast, the British have loved this region. The longing for sun, sea air and summer holidays attracted first the aristocracy and high society from grey Great Britain southwards – and later the painters and authors, the stars and the starlets were to follow. Among the most famous of the British coast dwellers today is the author Peter Mayle, who has devoted several books to the convergence of English eccentricity and French finesse. One of them bears the title "Hotel Pastis" – and John and Pauline Larkin's guest house owes its name to this work. The couple (how could it be otherwise!) came from London to St Tropez, and the former graphic designer and his wife have restored a Provençal villa in masterly fashion and given it a touch of the London lifestyle: they mix beds in the style of the French country house, Chinese wardrobes and design classics such as those by Mies van der Rohe, adding opulent mirrors, mighty copper bathtubs and modern art prints by Hockney and Lichtenstein. All rooms offer a patio, a balcony or a terrace; the wonderful veranda outside room 4 measures nearly 200 square feet and looks out over the pool to the sea. With their relaxed "no dress code" approach the Larkins remain true to British habits – but they serve breakfast à la française and in doing so make guests of all other nationalities happy.

Book to pack: "Hotel Pastis" by Peter Mayle.

Pastis Hôtel St Tropez
61 Avenue du Général Leclerc
83990 St Tropez
France
Tel. +33 4 9812 5650
Fax +33 4 9496 9982
reception@pastis-st-tropez.com
www.pastis-st-tropez.com
**Open from the end of December
to the end of November**

DIRECTIONS	110 yards from the sea, 550 yards from the old harbour. 56 miles southwest of Nice Airport.
RATES	€€
ROOMS	9 rooms.
FOOD	The owners serve breakfast and offer good tips for restaurants.
HISTORY	The villa was built at the beginning of the 20th century as a private house and later served as a hotel. John and Pauline Larkin discovered the dilapidated property in 2002 and completely redesigned it.
X-FACTOR	The pool, exquisitely lined with marble tiles in black, dark green and dark grey.

Little London in St. Tropez

Seit der schottische Schriftsteller Tobias Smollett Mitte des 18. Jahrhunderts seine Reisebriefe aus Südeuropa mit vielen lobenden Zeilen über die französische Küste veröffentlicht hat, lieben die Briten diese Region. Die Sehnsucht nach Sonne, Seeluft und Sommerfrische ließ zunächst Adel und High Society aus dem grauen Großbritannien gen Süden ziehen – später folgten die Maler und Schriftsteller, Stars und Sternchen. Zu den berühmtesten britischen Küstenbewohnern heute zählt der Autor Peter Mayle, der dem Zusammentreffen englischer Exzentrik und französischer Finesse mehrere Bücher gewidmet hat. Eines davon trägt den Titel »Hotel Pastis« – ihm verdankt das charmante Gästehaus von John und Pauline Larkin seinen Namen, die (wie könnte es anders sein!) aus London nach St. Tropez kamen. Der ehemalige Grafikdesigner und seine Frau haben eine provenzalische Villa gekonnt restauriert und ihr einen Touch Londoner Lifestyle verliehen: Sie mischen Betten im französischen Landhausstil, chinesische Schränke sowie Designklassiker wie von Mies van der Rohe und addieren opulente Spiegel, mächtige Kupferwannen und moderne Kunstdrucke von Hockney und Lichtenstein. Alle Räume bieten einen Patio, einen Balkon oder eine Terrasse; die wunderbare Veranda vor Zimmer 4 misst sogar 18 Quadratmeter und blickt auf den Pool und bis zum Meer. Mit einem entspannten »no dress code« bleiben die Larkins britischen Gewohnheiten treu – das Frühstück servieren sie aber à la française und machen damit Gäste aller anderen Nationalitäten glücklich.

Buchtipp: »Hotel Pastis« von Peter Mayle.

Little London à Saint-Tropez

Depuis que l'écrivain écossais Tobias Smollett a publié au milieu du XVIIIe siècle ses récits de voyage sur l'Europe du Sud, ne tarissant pas d'éloges sur la Côte d'Azur, les Britanniques sont devenus des inconditionnels de cette région. Le désir de soleil, d'air marin et de vacances a tout d'abord incité les nobles et la High Society à quitter la Grande-Bretagne brumeuse pour le Midi, plus tard les peintres et écrivains, stars et starlettes les ont rejoints. L'auteur Peter Mayle est aujourd'hui l'un des plus célèbres résidents britanniques de la Côte, où il a commencé à écrire une série de livres sur la rencontre entre l'excentricité britannique et le raffinement français. « Hôtel Pastis », un de ses best-sellers, a inspiré deux Londoniens, John et Pauline Larkin, venus s'installer (bien évidemment !) à Saint-Tropez et qui ont donné le nom de ce roman à leur charmant hôtel. L'ancien graphiste et sa femme ont admirablement restauré cette villa provençale et lui ont conféré une touche de Lifestyle londonien. Ils combinent les lits de campagne, les armoires chinoises ainsi que des classiques du design comme ceux de Mies van der Rohe, ajoutant des miroirs opulents, des baignoires en cuivre imposantes et des reproductions modernes de Hockney et Lichtenstein. Toutes les pièces disposent d'un patio, d'un balcon ou d'une terrasse, la splendide véranda de la chambre 4 mesure même 18 mètres carrés et donne sur la piscine et sur la mer. L'ambiance y est détendue, les Larkin restent fidèles aux habitudes britanniques du « no dress code ». Toutefois, le petit déjeuner est français pour contenter les clients de toutes nationalités.

Livre à emporter : « Hôtel Pastis » de Peter Mayle.

ANREISE	100 m vom Meer, 500 m vom alten Hafen entfernt. 90 km südwestlich vom Flughafen Nizza gelegen.
PREISE	€€
ZIMMER	9 Zimmer.
KÜCHE	Die Besitzer servieren Frühstück und verraten gute Tipps für Restaurants.
GESCHICHTE	Die Villa wurde Anfang des 20. Jahrhunderts als Privathaus erbaut und diente später als Hotel. John und Pauline Larkin entdeckten das baufällige Anwesen 2002 und gestalteten es rundum neu.
X-FAKTOR	Der raffiniert mit Marmorfliesen in Schwarz, Dunkelgrün und Dunkelgrau ausgekleidete Pool.

ACCÈS	À 100 m de la mer, à 500 m du vieux port. Situé à 90 km au sud-ouest de l'aéroport de Nice.
PRIX	€€
CHAMBRES	9 chambres.
RESTAURATION	Les propriétaires servent le petit déjeuner et communiquent de bonnes adresses de restaurants.
HISTOIRE	La villa, maison particulière à l'origine, a été construite au début du XXe siècle. Elle a été transformée plus tard en hôtel. John et Pauline Larkin ont découvert cette propriété vétuste en 2002 et l'ont complètement restaurée.
LES « PLUS »	La belle piscine au carrelage de marbre noir, vert et gris foncés.

Once in a Lifetime
Hôtel du Cap-Eden-Roc, Cap d'Antibes

Hôtel du Cap-Eden-Roc, Cap d'Antibes

Once in a Lifetime

Sometimes you allow yourself to dream of holidays as they are portrayed in cinema: of a cream-coloured palace by the sea, a perfectly manicured park through which a path leads like a catwalk to the coast, a rocky pool on whose edge you sunbathe in the current season's Eres bikini. You dream, too, of suites in the Louis XVI style, a restaurant whose terraces recall the deck of a yacht, a piano bar in which the barkeeper can tell at a glance what your favourite drink is. Wistful dreams may lead you to the Hôtel du Cap-Eden-Roc, because this hotel is cinema – during the Cannes Film Festival, indeed, it is truly great cinema. At this time the likes of Matt Damon and Leonardo DiCaprio, Cate Blanchett and Meryl Streep, Dustin Hoffman and Sean Connery turn up in a steady parade – the visitors' book reads like Hollywood's premier cast list. In contrast to film studios, however, there is no void behind the scenes here: the elegant establishment on the Cap d'Antibes celebrates the old-school hotel business and is the loveliest symbol of the classic summer resort. Until a few years ago the rooms got by without a television, hairdryers were brought only when requested and credit cards were not accepted – what counted then and still counts today is the personal and, it goes without saying, extremely discreet service. This is to be enjoyed in its most perfect form in a junior suite with a terrace and a sea view – lower categories of room are out of the question here. After all, you should make no compromises when you dream.

Book to pack: "Tender is the Night" by F. Scott Fitzgerald (the Hôtel du Cap-Eden-Roc was the inspiration for the "Hôtel des Etrangers").

Hôtel du Cap-Eden-Roc	
Boulevard JF Kennedy, BP 29	
06601 Antibes	
France	
Tel. +33 4 9361 3901	
Fax +33 4 9367 7604	
reservation@hdcer.com	
www.hotel-du-cap-eden-roc.com	
Open from mid-April to mid-October	

DIRECTIONS	Some 16 miles south of Nice Airport.
RATES	€€€€
ROOMS	59 rooms and 60 suites in the main building, the "Eden Roc" pavilion and the "Deux Fontaines" residence, 1 villa.
FOOD	The "Eden Roc" serves Mediterranean cuisine, the "Grill" tapas and sushi. In addition there are two bars.
HISTORY	The original "Villa Soleil" was built in 1870 by the publisher of "Le Figaro" as an authors' retreat. Since 1887 the complex has been a hotel.
X-FACTOR	The enchanting cabanas in the cliffs make up for the missing beach.

Einmal im Leben

Manchmal darf man von Ferien wie im Kino träumen: Von einem cremefarbenen Palast am Meer, einem makellos manikürten Park, durch den ein Weg wie ein Laufsteg zur Küste führt, einem Felsenpool, an dessen Rand man im Eres-Bikini der aktuellen Saison sonnenbadet. Von Suiten im Louis-XVI-Stil, einem Restaurant, dessen Terrasse ans Deck einer Jacht erinnert, einer Pianobar, in der dem Barkeeper ein einziger Blick genügt, um den Lieblingsdrink zu kennen. Besonders sehnsüchtige Träume dürfen einen ins Hôtel du Cap-Eden-Roc führen, denn dieses Hotel ist Kino – während des Filmfestivals in Cannes sogar ganz großes Kino. Dann geben sich hier Matt Damon und Leonardo DiCaprio, Cate Blanchett und Meryl Streep, Dustin Hoffman und Sean Connery die Klinke in die Hand – das Gästebuch liest sich wie Hollywoods beste Besetzungsliste. Im Gegensatz zu Filmstudios herrscht hier aber hinter den Kulissen keine Leere: Das elegante Haus am Cap d'Antibes zelebriert die Hotellerie alter Schule und ist das schönste Symbol der klassischen Sommerfrische. Bis vor wenigen Jahren kamen die Zimmer ohne Fernseher aus, Haartrockner wurden nur auf Wunsch gebracht und Kreditkarten nicht akzeptiert – was zählte und immer noch zählt, ist ein höchstpersönlicher und selbstverständlich höchst diskreter Service. Formvollendet genießt man ihn in einer Junior-Suite mit Terrasse und Meerblick, niedrigere Zimmerkategorien kommen hier nicht in Frage – beim Träumen sollte man keine Kompromisse eingehen.

Buchtipp: »Zärtlich ist die Nacht« von F. Scott Fitzgerald. (Das Hôtel du Cap-Eden-Roc war Vorbild für das »Hôtel des Etrangers«.)

Une fois dans sa vie

Des vacances de rêve comme au cinéma : un palace de couleur crème en bord de mer, un parc impeccable traversé par un chemin qui ressemblerait à un podium conduisant à la mer, une piscine à débordement creusée dans le rocher, au bord de laquelle on prendrait le soleil en bikini Eres dernier modèle. Des suites style Louis XVI, un restaurant dont la terrasse rappellerait le pont d'un yacht, un piano-bar où le barman sait en un coup d'œil quel est votre cocktail favori. Grand écran pour l'Hôtel du Cap-Eden-Roc : cet hôtel, très prisé par les stars du septième art pendant le Festival de Cannes, est un véritable programme. Matt Damon et Leonardo DiCaprio, Cate Blanchett et Meryl Streep, Dustin Hoffman et Sean Connery y défilent alors et le livre d'or se lit comme la meilleure des distributions d'Hollywood. Toutefois, contrairement aux studios de cinéma, les coulisses ne sont pas vides : cette majestueuse propriété du Cap d'Antibes qui célèbre une hôtellerie de la vieille école est le plus beau symbole des vacances très Riviera années 1950. Il y a quelques années encore, il n'y avait pas de télévision dans les chambres, les sèche-cheveux étaient fournis sur commande et les cartes de crédit n'étaient pas acceptées. Le plus important était et est toujours un service personnalisé haut de gamme et naturellemment d'une extrême discrétion. La perfection s'apprécie dans une suite Junior avec terrasse donnant sur la mer et il ne saurait être question de chambres à meilleur prix, car rien ne sert de faire des compromis quand on veut aller jusqu'au bout de ses rêves.

Livre à emporter : « Tendre est la nuit » de F. Scott Fitzgerald. (L'Hôtel du Cap-Eden-Roc a servi de modèle pour l'« Hôtel des Etrangers »).

ANREISE	25 km südlich vom Flughafen Nizza gelegen.
PREISE	€€€€
ZIMMER	59 Zimmer und 60 Suiten im Hauptbau, dem »Eden Roc«-Pavillon und der Residenz »Deux Fontaines«, 1 Villa.
KÜCHE	Das »Eden Roc« serviert mediterrane Küche, der »Grill« Tapas und Sushi. Zudem gibt es zwei Bars.
GESCHICHTE	1870 wurde die ursprüngliche »Villa Soleil« vom Verleger des »Figaro« als Autorenrefugium erbaut. Seit 1887 ist der Komplex ein Hotel.
X-FAKTOR	Den fehlenden Strand machen zauberhafte Cabanas in den Felsen wett.

ACCÈS	À 25 km au sud de l'aéroport de Nice.
PRIX	€€€€
CHAMBRES	59 chambres et 60 suites dans le bâtiment principal, le pavillon « Eden Roc » et la résidence « Les Deux Fontaines », 1 villa.
RESTAURATION	L'« Eden Roc » sert une cuisine méditerranéenne, le « Grill » des tapas et des sushis. Il y a en outre deux bars.
HISTOIRE	La « Villa Soleil » a été construite en 1870, par l'éditeur du Figaro, pour servir de refuge aux auteurs. Le complexe est un hôtel depuis 1887.
LES « PLUS »	De charmantes cabanes dans les rochers compensent l'absence de plage.

A Walk by the Water
Cap Estel, Eze-Bord-de-Mer

Cap Estel, Eze-Bord-de-Mer

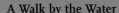

A Walk by the Water

The Cap Estel looks back on an illustrious list of owners: the property was founded by Frank Harris – the Irish journalist, a friend of Oscar Wilde's, transformed a former pig farm into a guest house here in 1900. Later on, a wealthy French lady bought the plot and lived on it with one of the last Counts Stroganoff – the couple was followed by Andreas Embiricos, the heir to a Greek ship-owning dynasty and an amateur poet in André Breton's circle. They all loved the cape for its breathtaking location and its privacy – on both counts it is still almost without equal. The Cap Estel stands imposingly on a peninsula between Nice and Monte Carlo; from its four villas, which afford the impression of a billion-aire's coastal retreat, fabulous views of the Mediterranean Sea unfold. Closest to the water are the suites of "La Mer", just across the sandy private beach – those who prefer to look out onto greenery rather than the blue of the sea should reserve the junior suite in "Le Parc". Its patio lies in the shade of an ancient tree – in 1911 a gardener had the Ficus macrophylla, at the time already weighing 3368 pounds, delivered in a container, and his courage in importing sensi-tive flora was rewarded by winning a local competition. Meanwhile the Cap Estel's head chef also grows vegetables and herbs in the park for dishes whose lightness inspires enthusiasm even in the most figure-conscious of the hotel's Hollywood clientele – the roll call of today's celebrity guests in no way taking second place to the list of former owners.
Books to pack: "My Life and Loves" by Frank Harris and "Amour Amour" by Andreas Embiricos.

Cap Estel

1312, Avenue Raymond Poincaré
06360 Eze-Bord-de-Mer
France
Tel. +33 4 9376 2929
Fax +33 4 9301 5520
contact@capestel.com
www.capestel.com
Open all year round

DIRECTIONS	Somewhat hidden and barely signposted below the medieval village of Eze, some 13 miles west of Nice Airport.
RATES	€€€€
ROOMS	4 rooms, 14 suites.
FOOD	The aromatic Mediterranean cuisine is served in the pool house or in your room.
HISTORY	The Cap Estel was opened in 2004 and completely reno-vated in 2009.
X-FACTOR	The saltwater pool, which appears to float spectacularly above the coast.

Dem Meer so nah

Es ist eine illustre Gesellschaft von Besitzern, auf die das Cap Estel zurückblickt: Gegründet wurde das Anwesen von Frank Harris – der irische Journalist und Freund Oscar Wildes verwandelte hier 1900 eine ehemalige Schweinefarm in ein Gästehaus. Später kaufte eine reiche Französin das Grundstück und bewohnte es mit einem der letzten Grafen Stroganoff – dem Paar folgte Andreas Embiricos, Erbe einer griechischen Schiffseignerdynastie und Hobbydichter im Zirkel André Bretons. Sie alle liebten das Kap wegen seiner atemberaubenden Lage und Privatsphäre – in beiden Bereichen ist es noch immer nahezu ohne Konkurrenz. Das Cap Estel thront auf einer Halbinsel zwischen Nizza und Monte Carlo; seine vier Villen wirken wie mediterrane Refugien eines Milliardärs und eröffnen sagenhafte Aussichten aufs Mittelmeer. Der See am nächsten sind die Suiten von »La Mer« über dem privaten Sandstrand – wer statt aufs Blau ins Grüne blicken möchte, sollte die Junior Suite im »Le Parc« reservieren. Ihr Patio liegt im Schatten eines uralten Baumes – 1911 ließ ein Gärtner den schon damals 1.800 Kilo schweren Ficus macrophylla in einem Container anliefern und gewann für seinen Mut beim Import empfindlicher Pflanzen einen lokalen Wettbewerb. Im Park kultiviert der Chefkoch von Cap Estel inzwischen auch Gemüse und Kräuter für Menüs, von deren Leichtigkeit selbst die figurbewusste Hollywood-Klientel des Hotels schwärmt – die Liste der heutigen prominenten Gäste steht der Liste der ehemaligen Besitzer in nichts nach.

Buchtipps: »Mein Leben und Lieben« von Frank Harris und »Amour Amour« von Andreas Embiricos.

Ceinturé par la mer

Le Cap Estel a vu défiler une illustre lignée de propriétaires : la propriété vit le jour grâce à Frank Harris, journaliste irlandais et ami d'Oscar Wilde, qui transforma ici en 1900 une ancienne porcherie en hôtel. Plus tard, le domaine fut racheté par une riche Française qui l'habita avec l'un des derniers comtes Stroganoff, suivi ensuite Andreas Embiricos, l'héritier d'une dynastie d'armateurs grecs et poète amateur dans le cercle d'André Breton. Tous aimaient le Cap pour sa situation géographique exceptionnelle et son intimité : dans ces deux domaines, il reste quasiment inégalé. Le Cap Estel trône sur une presqu'île entre Nice et Monte Carlo ; ses quatre villas ont l'air d'être les refuges d'un milliardaire en Méditerranée et disposent toutes d'une vue sublime sur la mer. Les suites « La Mer » dominent la plage de sable privée et sont au plus près des vagues ; si vous préférez la verdure, réservez la suite Junior du site « Le Parc ». Son patio est ombragé par un arbre centenaire. En 1911, un jardinier avait fait livrer dans un container un Ficus macrophylla de 1 800 kilo et avait ainsi remporté un concours local récompensant son audace pour avoir importé des plantes aussi délicates. Entre-temps, le chef cuisinier cultive aussi des légumes et des herbes aromatiques dans le parc de Cap Estel. Ils entrent dans la composition de ses menus, dont la légèreté ravit même une clientèle hollywoodienne soucieuse de garder la ligne. La liste des célébrités séjournant au Cap Estel de nos jours n'a rien à envier à celle des anciens propriétaires.

Livres à emporter : « My Life and Loves » de Frank Harris et « Amour Amour » d'Andreas Embiricos.

ANREISE	Etwas versteckt und kaum ausgeschildert unterhalb des mittelalterlichen Ortes Eze gelegen, 20 km westlich vom Flughafen Nizza gelegen.	ACCÈS	À l'abri des regards et pas très bien indiqué, situé en dessous du village médiéval d'Eze, à 20 km à l'ouest de l'aéroport de Nice.
PREISE	€€€€	PRIX	€€€€
ZIMMER	4 Zimmer, 14 Suiten.	CHAMBRES	4 chambres, 14 suites.
KÜCHE	Die aromatischen mediterranen Menüs werden im Poolhaus oder im Zimmer serviert.	RESTAURATION	Des menus méditerranéens sont servis au poolhouse ou dans les chambres.
GESCHICHTE	Das Cap Estel wurde 2004 eröffnet und 2009 rundum renoviert.	HISTOIRE	Le Cap Estel a ouvert ses portes en 2004 et a été entièrement rénové en 2009.
X-FAKTOR	Der Salzwasserpool, der spektakulär über der Küste zu schweben scheint.	LES « PLUS »	La piscine d'eau de mer semble flotter de manière spectaculaire au-dessus de la côte.

A Summer Retreat
Monte Carlo Beach, Monaco

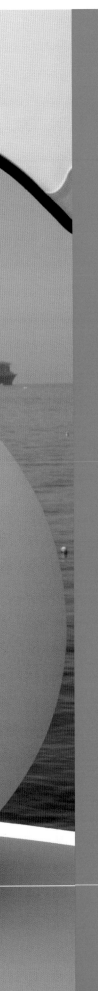

Monte Carlo Beach, Monaco

A Summer Retreat

She was considered the top high-society hostess and the best tabloid press journalist of the 1920s – the American Elsa Maxwell. When the rich and the beautiful of the world ceased using the Côte d'Azur merely as their winter quarters and discovered it as a summer travel destination, Monte Carlo was her patch: commissioned by the Société des Bains de Mer, she planned dance receptions and fancy-dress balls, organised garden parties and golf tournaments – always combined with invitations to the Monte Carlo Beach Hotel, which the architect Roger Séassal had just built. The Société did not fulfil her greatest wish – a sandy beach on a par with Venice's Lido – however they at least granted her a pool directly by the sea. After Elsa Maxwell's era the beach sand was poured on after all, and today it is possible to relax here in style and get a sense of the Côte d'Azur's legendary heyday. India Mahdavi has newly designed the 40 rooms and suites entirely in this spirit: inspired by the colours of the Riviera, the rooms present themselves in retro style, timelessly elegant and romantic at the same time and sensuously decorated with Matisse motifs and George Hoyningen-Huene's black-and-white photos of young women in bathing costumes. In the very elegant "Elsa" gourmet restaurant even the cuisine picks up the theme of the golden epoch of the Riviera – on the menu are dishes of the 1920s and 1930s, deliciously prepared with a modern twist. And the "Sea Lounge" by the water is among Monaco's best places for a party – Elsa Maxwell would be in her element.
Book to pack: "The Celebrity Circus" by Elsa Maxwell.

Monte Carlo Beach
c/o Monte-Carlo SBM
Place du Casino
98000 Monaco
Monaco
Tel. +377 9806 2525
Fax +377 9806 2626
resort@sbm.mc
www.monte-carlo-beach.com
Open from March to December

DIRECTIONS	Some 19 miles west of Nice Airport.
RATES	€€€€
ROOMS	26 rooms and 14 suites.
FOOD	Along with the "Elsa" and the "Sea Lounge" there is the relaxed "Le Deck" at the pool as well as the "La Vigie", open in summer with buffets at lunch- and dinnertime.
HISTORY	The completely renovated hotel opened in spring 2009. Even the gardens were designed anew – this task was undertaken by Jean Mus.
X-FACTOR	The "Sunshine" suite with private jacuzzi on the roof terrace.

Sommerfrische

Sie galt als erste Gastgeberin der High Society und beste Boulevardjournalistin der 1920er – die Amerikanerin Elsa Maxwell. Als die Reichen und Schönen der Welt die Côte d'Azur nicht mehr nur als Winterquartier nutzten, sondern auch als Reiseziel für den Sommer entdeckten, war Monte Carlo ihr Revier: Im Auftrag der Société des Bains de Mer plante sie Tanzfeste und Kostümbälle, organisierte Gartenpartys und Golfturniere – immer verbunden mit Einladungen ins Monte Carlo Beach Hotel, das der Architekt Roger Séassal gerade erbaut hatte. Ihren größten Wunsch – einen Sandstrand mit dem Flair des Lidos von Venedig – wollte ihr die Société nicht erfüllen, bewilligte aber zumindest einen Pool direkt am Meer. Nach Elsa Maxwells Ära wurde der Strand aber doch noch aufgeschüttet – heute entspannt man hier stilvoll und spürt den legendären Zeiten der Küste nach. Ganz in diesem Sinn hat India Mahdavi auch die 40 Zimmer und Suiten neu gestaltet: Inspiriert von den Farben der Riviera zeigen sich die Räume im Retro-Stil, zeitlos-elegant und romantisch zugleich und mit Matisse-Motiven sowie George Hoyningen-Huenes Schwarz-Weiß-Fotos von jungen Frauen in Badeanzügen sinnlich dekoriert. Sehr schick ist das Gourmet-Restaurant »Elsa«, in dem selbst die Küche die goldene Epoche der Riviera aufgreift – auf der Karte stehen Gerichte der 1920er und 1930er, die mit modernem Twist köstlich zubereitet werden. Und die »Sea Lounge« am Wasser gehört zu Monacos besten Partyplätzen – Elsa Maxwell wäre in ihrem Element.

Buchtipp: »Mein verrücktes Leben« von Elsa Maxwell.

Vacances monégasques

L'Américaine Elsa Maxwell, meilleure chroniqueuse des années 1920, était considérée comme « la plus parfaite des hôtesses ». Quand le Gotha, qui tenait ses quartiers d'hiver sur la Côte d'Azur, s'intéressa aussi à la saison estivale, Monte Carlo devint son quartier général. La Société des Bains de Mer la chargea d'organiser des fêtes et bals costumés, des garden-parties et des tournois de golf dont les invitations étaient toujours en rapport avec le Monte Carlo Beach Hotel, nouvellement construit par l'architecte Roger Séassal. Le souhait le plus cher d'Elsa, une plage de sable aussi belle que celle du Lido de Venise, ne sera tout d'abord pas réalisé, la Société des Bains de Mer préférant construire une piscine au bord de la mer. La plage de sable doré verra le jour, mais bien après l'ère d'Elsa Maxwell. De nos jours, on s'y détend tout en ressentant l'élégance d'antan. C'est dans cette optique qu'India Mahdavi a réaménagé les 40 chambres et suites : les pièces aux couleurs de la Riviera présentent un style rétro, à la fois élégant, intemporel et romantique et un décor sensuel avec des motifs de Matisse ainsi que des photographies en noir et blanc de George Hoyningen-Huenes représentant des jeunes filles en maillot de bain. Le restaurant gastronomique « Elsa », est également très chic et, lui aussi sous l'emprise de l'âge d'or de la Riviera, propose sur sa carte de délicieux plats des années 1920 et 1930 revisités tendance. Le « Sea Lounge », posé au bord de l'eau, est une des meilleures adresses de Monaco pour faire la fête : Elsa Maxwell serait tout à fait dans son élément.

Livre à emporter : « J'ai reçu le monde entier » d'Elsa Maxwell.

ANREISE	30 km westlich vom Flughafen Nizza gelegen.
PREISE	€€€€
ZIMMER	26 Zimmer und 14 Suiten.
KÜCHE	Neben dem »Elsa« und der »Sea Lounge« gibt es das legere »Le Deck« am Pool sowie das im Sommer geöffnete »La Vigie« mit Lunch- und Dinnerbuffets.
GESCHICHTE	Das rundum renovierte Hotel eröffnete im Frühjahr 2009. Selbst die Gärten wurden neu gestaltet – diesen Part übernahm Jean Mus.
X-FAKTOR	Die »Sunshine«-Suite mit privatem Jacuzzi auf der Dachterrasse.

ACCÈS	À 30 km à l'ouest de l'aéroport de Nice.
PRIX	€€€€
CHAMBRES	26 chambres et 14 suites.
RESTAURATION	Outre le « Elsa » et le « Sea Lounge », il existe encore « Le Deck » au bord de la piscine et « La Vigie » en été, qui sert des buffets midi et soir.
HISTOIRE	L'hôtel entièrement rénové a ouvert ses portes au printemps 2009. Même les jardins ont été réaménagés par Jean Mus.
LES « PLUS »	La suite « Sunshine » avec jacuzzi privatif sur la terrasse du toit.

The Island Scent
Casadelmar, Porto-Vecchio, Corsica

Casadelmar, Porto-Vecchio, Corsica

The Island Scent

With his eyes closed he could recognise his home from on board ship by its scent – this was the claim of none other than Napoléon Bonaparte, who was born in Corsica in 1769. Just following your nose is still possible here: particularly in spring an unforgettable aroma of the south and the sun hangs over the island, as at this time the maquis, the evergreen scrubby underbrush that covers about half of Corsica, is in bloom. The pleasures only increase in the garden of Hotel Casadelmar, in which cypresses, pines, orange and olive trees grow – as well as in the restaurant, whose Mediterranean cuisine transforms local herbs and spices, fish and seafood into sheer culinary joy. The architecture of Casadelmar is also marked by a closeness to nature and a love of the land. The Frenchman Jean-François Bodin has integrated the low building harmoniously into the coastal region of Porto-Vecchio, with cedar wood, grey stone and large windows constituting the design. Without exception, all rooms offer a sea view from private terraces – as does the spa and the spectacular pool, which shines blue during the day and shimmers like jade at night. In the rooms themselves clear lines dominate; a little vintage glamour is provided by such design classics as Le Corbusier's chaise longue or Knoll's Bertoia armchair. Fabrics in strawberry, lilac and honey tones once again take up the Corsican colour scheme – those nuances of nature when the maquis blooms in spring.

Book to pack: "Colomba" by Prosper Mérimée.

Casadelmar
Route de Palombaggia BP 93
20538 Porto-Vecchio Cedex
France
Tel. +33 495 723 434
Fax +33 495 723 435
info@casadelmar.fr
www.casadelmar.fr
**Open from the beginning of
April to the end of October**

DIRECTIONS	Located on the south coast above the bay of Porto-Vecchio. Figari Airport is 25 min away.
RATES	€€€
ROOMS	14 rooms and 20 suites (of which 3 suites are in a separate villa, the whole of which can also be rented).
FOOD	Alongside the "Casadelmar" gourmet restaurant there is also the "Restaurant Grill" with pool bar.
HISTORY	The hotel was opened in May 2004.
X-FACTOR	The private beach with wooden decks, smart red loungers and straw-covered sunshades.

Der Duft der Insel

Er könne seine Heimat schon vom Schiff aus mit geschlossenen Augen am Duft erkennen, behauptete einst Napoléon Bonaparte, der 1769 auf Korsika zur Welt kam. Der Nase nach reisen – das ist hier noch immer möglich: Vor allem im Frühling liegt ein unvergleichliches Aroma nach Süden und Sonne über der Insel, denn dann blüht die Macchia, die immergrüne Wald- und Buschfläche, die rund die Hälfte Korsikas bedeckt. Steigern lässt sich dieser Genuss in den Gärten des Hotels Casadelmar, in denen Zypressen, Pinien, Orangen- und Olivenbäume wachsen – sowie im Restaurant, dessen mediterrane Küche einheimische Kräuter und Gewürze, Fisch und Meeresfrüchte in Gaumenglück verwandelt. Nähe zur Natur und Liebe zum Land zeichnen auch die Architektur des Casadelmar aus. Der Franzose Jean-François Bodin hat den flachen Bau harmonisch mit der Küstenregion von Porto-Vecchio verbunden und ihn aus Zedernholz, grauem Stein und großen Fenstern gestaltet. Wirklich alle Zimmer bieten von privaten Terrassen aus Meerblick – ebenso wie das Spa und der spektakuläre Pool, der tagsüber blau leuchtet und nachts wie Jade schimmert. In den Räumen selbst dominieren klare Linien; für etwas Vintage-Glamour sorgen Designklassiker wie Le Corbusiers Chaiselongue oder der Bertoia-Sessel von Knoll. Und Stoffe in Erdbeer-, Flieder- und Honigtönen greifen die Farben Korsikas wieder auf – die Nuancen der Natur, wenn im Frühling die Macchia blüht.

Buchtipp: »Colomba« von Prosper Mérimée.

Le parfum de l'île

Passant en bateau au large de la Corse, Napoléon Bonaparte (né sur l'île en 1769) affirmait pouvoir reconnaître sa patrie, les yeux fermés, à son parfum particulier. Voyager en sentant les odeurs, c'est toujours possible sur l'île de beauté : surtout au printemps quand une odeur incomparable, celle du Midi et du soleil, embaume toute la Corse. C'est la saison où le maquis, cette forêt dense et verte d'arbrisseaux qui couvre la moitié de la surface de l'île, est en fleur. Le parfum s'intensifie encore dans les jardins de l'hôtel Casadelmar où poussent cyprès, pins, orangers et oliviers – ainsi qu'au restaurant de l'hôtel dont la cuisine méditerranéenne transforme les herbes et épices, poissons et fruits de mer locaux en un vrai régal. La proximité avec la nature et l'amour de la terre caractérisent aussi l'architecture de Casadelmar. Jean-François Bodin a conçu ce bâtiment plat en totale harmonie avec la région côtière de Porto-Vecchio en le dotant de bois de cèdre, de pierres grises et de grandes baies vitrées. Toutes les chambres ont vue sur la mer depuis leur terrasse privée, tout comme le spa et la piscine spectaculaire, bleue de jour et jade de nuit. Dans les chambres elles-mêmes, les lignes claires dominent ; des classiques du design comme la chaise longue de Le Corbusier et le fauteuil Bertoia de Knoll apportent un peu de glamour vintage. Les tissus dans les tons de fraise, lilas et miel reprennent les couleurs de la Corse : celles de la nature au printemps quand le maquis fleurit.

Livre à emporter : « Colomba » de Prosper Mérimée.

ANREISE	An der Südostküste über der Bucht von Porto-Vecchio gelegen. Der Flughafen Figari ist 25 min entfernt.	ACCÈS	Sur la côte sud-est, surplombant la baie de Porto-Vecchio. L'aéroport Figari est à 25 min.
PREISE	€€€	PRIX	€€€
ZIMMER	14 Zimmer und 20 Suiten (davon 3 Suiten in einer separaten Villa, die auch komplett gemietet werden kann).	CHAMBRES	14 chambres et 20 suites (dont 3 suites dans une villa à part, qui peut être aussi entièrement louée).
KÜCHE	Neben dem Gourmet-Restaurant »Casadelmar« gibt es das »Restaurant Grill« mit Poolbar.	RESTAURATION	Outre le restaurant gastronomique « Casadelmar », vous trouverez le « Restaurant Grill » avec bar-piscine.
GESCHICHTE	Das Hotel wurde im Mai 2004 eröffnet.	HISTOIRE	L'hôtel a ouvert ses portes en mai 2004.
X-FAKTOR	Der Privatstrand mit Holzdecks, schicken roten Liegen und strohgedeckten Sonnenschirmen.	LES « PLUS »	La plage privée avec sa terrasse en bois, ses chaises longues rouges ultra chic et ses parasols en paille.

For Stellar Moments
Stella Maris, Punta Chiappa

Stella Maris, Punta Chiappa

For Stellar Moments

A house at the end of the world, as it were – the only building on a dramatic coast whose cliffs drop steeply into the sea, standing in the shade of ancient chestnut and walnut trees with a view of a sunset that is the epitome of beauty and longing: for a late Romantic like Lord Byron, the Stella Maris must have been a place of spiritual kinship. The British poet and dandy, whose life and work were as successful as they were eccentric, came to this small hotel on the Cape of Portofino in 1821 and wrote passionate lines of verse about the overwhelming scenery around him. The Stella Maris has not only preserved the sensual atmosphere of these days but also stylishly modernised it. The hotel is still accessible only by boat; the nearest neighbours live completely out of sight, and within the colourful walls of the interior antiques and new furnishings are combined with elegance and charm. A room facing the sea is naturally a must – the best ones also have access to the enchanted garden, in which orchids and passion flowers bloom. The hotel restaurant is among the region's most sought-after establishments. On cool days you sit in the bright dining hall; in summer you enjoy every moment on the idyllic terrace with a panoramic view across the Golfo Paradiso: fresh seasonal dishes are served here by candlelight while above the Stella Maris, the "star of the sea", the stars twinkle in the Ligurian sky.

Book to pack: "Childe Harold's Pilgrimage" by Lord Byron.

Stella Maris
Via S. Nicolò 68
Punta Chiappa
16032 Camogli
Italy
Tel. +39 0185 770 285 and +39 0331 261 417
Fax +39 0331 264 864
stellamaris@cssitalia.it
www.stellamaris.cc
Open all year round

DIRECTIONS	Camogli lies 22 miles away from Genoa; from the harbour the transfer by boat takes 10 min, the ascent up stone steps to the hotel about 7 min.
RATES	€ (minimum length of stay 2 nights).
ROOMS	9 rooms, 2 suites.
FOOD	Only ingredients from the region are used for the simple yet tasty Ligurian fare.
HISTORY	The entire hotel was newly renovated at the beginning of 2009.
X-FACTOR	Divers find fascinating spots with corals here.

Für Sternstunden

Ein Haus gleichsam am Ende der Welt – als einziges Gebäude an einer dramatischen Küste gelegen, deren Felsen
steil ins Meer stürzen, im Schatten uralter Kastanien- und
Walnussbäume stehend und mit Blick in einen Sonnenuntergang, der ein Inbegriff von Schönheit und Sehnsucht
ist: Für einen Spätromantiker wie Lord Byron muss das
Stella Maris ein Ort wie eine Seelenverwandtschaft gewesen
sein. Der britische Dichter und Dandy, der sein Leben und
Werk ebenso erfolgreich wie exzentrisch inszenierte, kam 1821
in dieses kleine Hotel am Kap von Portofino und widmete
der überwältigenden Szenerie ringsum leidenschaftliche
Verszeilen. Die sinnliche Atmosphäre dieser Tage hat das
Stella Maris bis heute behalten und sehr stilvoll moderni-
siert. Das Haus ist noch immer nur per Boot erreichbar, die
nächsten Nachbarn wohnen außerhalb jeglicher Sichtweite,
und im Inneren werden vor farbigen Wänden Antiquitäten
und neues Mobiliar mit Chic und Charme kombiniert. Ein
Zimmer zum Meer ist hier natürlich unverzichtbar – die
besten Räume haben zudem Zugang zum verwunschenen
Garten, in dem Orchideen und Passionsblumen gedeihen.
Das Restaurant des Hotels gehört zu den begehrtesten
Adressen der Region. An kühlen Tagen sitzt man im hellen
Speisesaal, im Sommer genießt man jede Sekunde auf
der stimmungsvollen Terrasse mit Panoramablick über
den Golfo Paradiso: Hier werden die frischen saisonalen
Menüs im Kerzenschein serviert, und über dem Stella
Maris, dem »Stern des Meeres«, funkeln die Sterne am
Himmel über Ligurien.
Buchtipp: »Childe Harolds Pilgerfahrt« von Lord Byron.

Heures étoilées

Une maison pour ainsi dire au bout du monde. Seul bâtiment situé dans un décor dramatique, sur une côte bordée
de falaises à pic, il se dresse à l'ombre de châtaigniers et de
noyers centenaires et donne sur un coucher de soleil, incar-
nation de la beauté et de la nostalgie. Rien d'étonnant à ce
qu'un romantique comme Lord Byron ait eu des affinités
avec le Stella Maris. Le poète et dandy britannique, qui mit
en scène sa vie et son œuvre de manière aussi brillante
qu'excentrique, séjourna dans ce petit hôtel du golfe de
Portofino en 1821 et consacra des vers passionnés à ce décor
impressionnant. Le Stella Maris a conservé l'ambiance sen-
suelle de cette époque et l'a modernisée avec beaucoup d'élégance. La maison n'est toujours accessible que par bateau et
les voisins ne sont toujours pas en vue aux alentours. Ses
intérieurs combinent avec charme et élégance des antiquités
et du mobilier contemporain sur fond de murs colorés. Une
chambre avec vue sur la mer est naturellement un must. Les
meilleures chambres ont, en outre, accès au fabuleux jardin
où poussent orchidées et passiflores. Le restaurant de l'hôtel
fait partie des adresses les plus courues de la région. Par
temps frais, vous dînerez dans une salle à manger lumineuse
mais, en été, vous profiterez de chaque seconde sur la terrasse,
dans ce cadre poétique avec vue sur le Golfo Paradiso. Vous
y apprécierez des menus de saison à base de produits frais
et servis à la lueur de chandelles, sous un ciel constellé
d'étoiles brillant au-dessus du Stella Maris, « l'étoiles des
mers » de Ligurie.
**Livre à emporter : « Le pèlerinage du chevalier Harold » de
Lord Byron.**

ANREISE	Camogli liegt 35 km von Genua entfernt; vom Hafen aus dauert der Bootstransfer 10 min, der Aufstieg zum Hotel über Steintreppen etwa 7 min.
PREISE	€ (2 Nächte Mindestaufenthalt).
ZIMMER	9 Zimmer, 2 Suiten.
KÜCHE	Für die ligurische Hausmannskost werden nur Zutaten aus der Region verwendet.
GESCHICHTE	Das gesamte Hotel wurde Anfang 2009 renoviert.
X-FAKTOR	Taucher finden hier faszinierende Korallen-Spots.

ACCÈS	Camogli est à 35 km de Gênes ; la traversée en bateau, depuis le port, dure 10 min, la montée des marches en pierre jusqu'à l'hôtel environ 7 min.
PRIX	€ (durée minimum de séjour de 2 nuits).
CHAMBRES	9 chambres, 2 suites.
RESTAURATION	Pour les plats traditionnels liguriens, seuls des produits frais de la région sont utilisés.
HISTOIRE	L'hôtel a été entièrement rénové début 2009.
LES « PLUS »	Les plongeurs y trouveront de magnifiques coraux.

Bella Italia
Hotel Splendido, Portofino

Hotel Splendido, Portofino

Bella Italia

Portofino is one of those places whose very name conjures up an image in your mind's eye – even if you have never been there. Fishermen's houses in ochre, terracotta and saffron; green hills plunging steeply into the sparkling sea; piazzas and marinas – the Italian Riviera is concentrated here in such a small area that it could be a film set. Perhaps that is why Hollywood feels so at home here: once Humphrey Bogart and Lauren Bacall, Roberto Rossellini and Ingrid Bergman, Richard Burton and Elizabeth Taylor came to Portofino; today it is Barbra Streisand, Robert de Niro and George Clooney. They all stayed, and continue to stay, in the Hotel Splendido, which stands high on the slope and enjoys a view as suitable for the silver screen as Portofino has to offer. A room overlooking the sea with a balcony is a must: the best ones are the newly renovated junior suites, which spoil guests not only with a breathtaking view but also with parquet floors, classic furniture in cream tones and fresh cut flowers. When it comes to the panorama, the hotel pool is second to none – in addition it is filled with salt water, kept at a constant 30 degrees and overseen by a pool butler who will deliver guests' every whim and wish to the sun lounger, from favourite reading matter to face spray. Admittedly, all this comes at a price. But those who cannot travel to Portofino should hold on to the image that comes to mind as soon as they hear the name. It is still enchanting – and completely free of charge.

Books to pack: "Satura" by Eugenio Montale and "The Path to the Spiders' Nests" by Italo Calvino.

Hotel Splendido
Salita Baratta, 16
16034 Portofino
Italy
Tel. +39 0185 267 801
Fax +39 0185 267 806
info@splendido.net
www.hotelsplendido.com
**Open from the beginning of April
to the beginning of November**

DIRECTIONS	10 min on foot from the town centre. The distance to Genoa Airport is 23 miles.
RATES	€€€€
ROOMS	29 rooms and 35 suites, designed by Michel Jouannet.
FOOD	Along with the Italian "La Terrazza" there is the informal "Pool Restaurant".
HISTORY	In the 16th century the building served as a monastery, in the 19th century it became a private residence. In 1901 it opened as a hotel, and has been run by Orient Express since 1985.
X-FACTOR	The exceedingly discreet service.

Bella Italia

Portofino ist einer jener Orte, bei denen man ein Bild vor Augen hat, sobald man den Namen hört – selbst, wenn man noch nie dort war. Fischerhäuser in Ocker, Terrakotta und Safran; grüne Hügel, die steil ins glitzernde Meer abfallen; Piazzas und Jachthäfen – die italienische Riviera auf wenig Raum so konzentriert zusammengefasst, als wäre sie eine Filmkulisse. Vielleicht fühlt sich Hollywood deshalb hier wie zu Hause: Nach Portofino kamen einst Humphrey Bogart und Lauren Bacall, Roberto Rossellini und Ingrid Bergman, Richard Burton und Elizabeth Taylor; heute sind es Barbra Streisand, Robert de Niro und George Clooney. Sie alle wohnten und wohnen im Hotel Splendido, das erhöht am Hang liegt und den leinwandtauglichsten Blick eröffnet, den Portofino zu bieten hat. Ein Zimmer zum Meer und mit Balkon ist ein Muss, am schönsten sind die frisch renovierten Junior-Suiten, die nicht nur mit einer atemberaubenden Aussicht, sondern auch mit Parkett, klassischen Möbeln in Cremetönen und frischen Blumen verwöhnen. Der Hotel-pool kann in puncto Panorama ebenfalls mithalten – und wird darüber hinaus mit Salzwasser gefüllt, konstant auf 30 Grad gehalten sowie von einem Badebutler betreut, der seinen Gästen von der Lieblingslektüre bis zum Gesichts-spray jeden Wunsch an die Sonnenliege bringt. Zugegeben: All das hat seinen Preis. Doch auch wer nicht nach Porto-fino reisen kann, sollte das Bild behalten, das er vor Augen hat, sobald er den Namen hört. Es ist zauberhaft – und kostenfrei.

Buchtipps: »Satura« von Eugenio Montale und »Wo Spinnen ihre Nester bauen« von Italo Calvino.

Bella Italia

Portofino est un de ces endroits que l'on se représente immédiatement dès que son nom est prononcé – même si l'on n'y a jamais mis les pieds. Des maisons de pêcheurs de couleur ocre, terracota et safran ; des collines vertes qui plongent dans une mer scintillante ; les piazzas et les ports de plaisance – la Riviera italienne concentrée sur si peu d'es-pace qu'on la prendrait pour un décor de cinéma. C'est peut-être la raison pour laquelle Hollywood se sent ici chez lui : Humphrey Bogart et Lauren Bacall, Roberto Rossellini et Ingrid Bergman, Richard Burton et Elizabeth Taylor étaient tous des habitués de Portofino ; aujourd'hui, on y croise Barbra Streisand, Robert de Niro et George Clooney. Tous avaient l'habitude de descendre ou descendent encore à l'hôtel Splendido, un hôtel prestigieux se dressant sur un promontoire et révélant le panorama le plus pittoresque de Portofino. Une chambre avec vue sur la mer est un must. Les suites Junior fraîchement rénovées sont les plus belles. Dotées d'une vue à couper le souffle, elles sont également élégamment garnies de parquet, de meubles classiques dans des tons de crème et décorées de beaux bouquets de fleurs. La piscine de l'hôtel jouit également d'une vue splendide sur la baie. Elle est remplie d'eau salée et chauffée en per-manence à 30°C. Un service personnalisé de majordome vous y est même proposé. Nul besoin de se lever de sa chaise longue, on exauce tous vos vœux, de la lecture à la crème solaire. Il faut avouer que tout cela a un prix. Toutefois, si vous ne pouvez pas vous rendre à Portofino, gardez l'image que vous en avez à l'évocation de son nom. Le charme opère toujours et c'est gratuit.

Livres à emporter : « Satura » d'Eugenio Montale et « Le sentier des nids d'araignées » d'Italo Calvino.

ANREISE	10 Gehminuten vom Ortskern entfernt. Die Distanz zum Flughafen Genua beträgt 37 km.
PREISE	€€€€
ZIMMER	29 Zimmer und 35 Suiten, designt von Michel Jouannet.
KÜCHE	Neben dem italienischen »La Terrazza« gibt es das lege-re »Pool Restaurant«.
GESCHICHTE	Im 16. Jahrhundert diente das Gebäude als Kloster, im 19. Jahrhundert wurde es eine Privatresidenz. 1901 eröff-nete es als Hotel, seit 1985 wird es von Orient-Express geführt.
X-FAKTOR	Der äußerst diskrete Service.

ACCÈS	À 10 min à pied du centre du village. L'aéroport de Gênes est à 37 km.
PRIX	€€€€
CHAMBRES	29 chambres et 35 suites, conçues par Michel Jouannet.
RESTAURATION	Outre « La Terrazza » aux spécialités italiennes, le « Pool Restaurant » propose des collations.
HISTOIRE	Monastère au XVIe siècle, le bâtiment est devenu une résidence privée au XIXe siècle. L'hôtel a ouvert ses portes en 1901 et il est dirigé par Orient-Express depuis 1985.
LES « PLUS »	Un service d'une extrême discrétion.

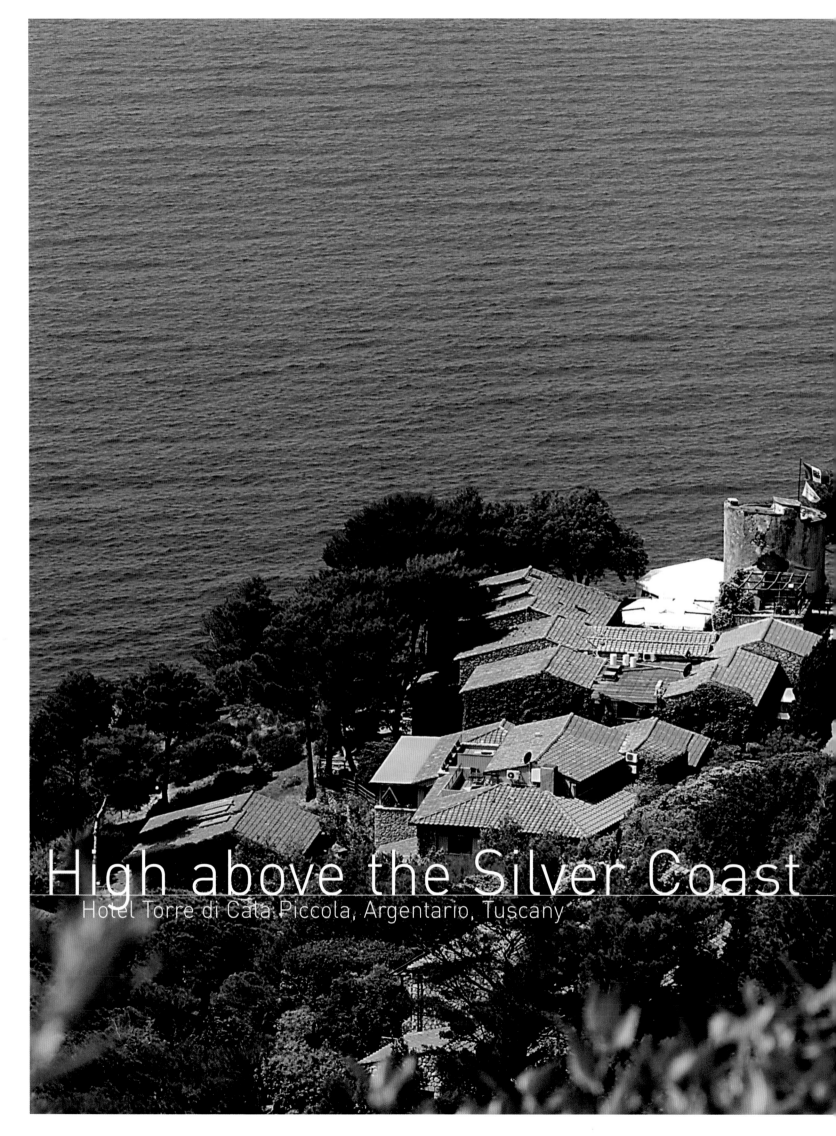

High above the Silver Coast

Hotel Torre di Cala Piccola, Argentario, Tuscany

Hotel Torre di Cala Piccola, Argentario, Tuscany

High above the Silver Coast

How Monte Argentario, the Silver Mountain, came by its name is a favourite topic amongst the locals, and one discussed with typical Italian passion. Some espouse the simple and, on sunny days, very plausible thesis that the name calls to mind the reflections of silvery light on the sea; others reach for the history books and point to an aristocratic family, the Domitii Ahenobarbi, who supported the Roman Republic as moneylenders ("argentarii") and received this region in return. Both parties, though, agree that Monte Argentario is one of the most glittering destinations of the Maremma: on the most spectacular coastal stretches of the former island, which is now connected to Italy's boot by means of three spits, stand numerous villas owned by the rich and the beautiful. But even those who have not risen to prominence in life can still live in a prominent location here – best of all in the Hotel Torre di Cala Piccola, standing proudly 330 feet above the sea a few miles from Porto Santo Stefano. Grouped around the ruins of a Spanish watchtower are houses made of local stone and wood, in whose rooms the rustic charm of the region has been preserved, albeit at the expense of opulent luxury. The most sought-after rooms look out onto the islands of Giglio, Giannutri and Montecristo; this beautiful panorama also presents itself from the restaurant garden and the freshwater pool. The private, wonderfully Italian rocky bay, complete with a bar and a restaurant, is an inviting place for a dip in crystal-clear salt water, the sea a sparkling silver, naturally.

Book to pack: "The Count of Monte Cristo" by Alexandre Dumas.

Hotel Torre di Cala Piccola

Argentario

58019 Porto Santo Stefano

Italy

Tel. +39 0564 825 111

Fax +39 0564 825 235

info@torredicalapiccola.com

www.torredicalapiccola.com

**Open from mid-March
to the end of October**

DIRECTIONS	5 miles from Porto Santo Stefano. Rome Airport is 90 miles away.
RATES	€€
ROOMS	50 rooms.
FOOD	The restaurant specialises in seafood.
HISTORY	The Spanish watchtower dates from the 17th century. Renovation work on parts of the approximately 30-year-old hotel is undertaken on a regular basis, most recently at the beginning of 2009.
X-FACTOR	A good place for amateur historians: many Etruscan excavation sites nearby.

Hoch über der Silberküste

Wie der Monte Argentario, der Silberberg, zu seinem Namen kam – das ist ein gerne und mit italienischer Leidenschaft diskutiertes Thema unter den Einheimischen. Die einen vertreten die simple und an Sonnentagen sehr einleuchtende These, der Name erinnere an die silbrigen Lichtreflexe auf dem Meer; die anderen verweisen auf die Geschichte und die Adelsfamilie der Domitii Ahenobarbi, welche die römische Republik als Darlehensgeber (»argentarii«) unterstützte und im Gegenzug dieses Gebiet erhielt. Einig sind sich beide Parteien aber immerhin darüber, dass der Monte Argentario eines der glanzvollsten Ziele der Maremma ist: An den spektakulärsten Küstenabschnitten der einstigen Insel, die heute über drei Landzungen mit dem Stiefel verbunden ist, stehen zahlreiche Villen der Reichen und Schönen. Doch auch wer nicht prominent ist, kann hier in prominenter Lage wohnen – am besten im Hotel Torre di Cala Piccola, das 100 Meter hoch über dem Meer, einige Kilometer von Porto Santo Stefano entfernt, thront. Rund um die Ruine eines spanischen Wachturms gruppieren sich Häuser aus einheimischem Stein und Holz, in deren Zimmern man auf opulenten Luxus verzichtet und stattdessen den rustikalen Charme der Region bewahrt hat. Die begehrtesten Räume schauen auf die Inseln Giglio, Giannutri und Montecristo; dieses wunderschöne Panorama eröffnen auch der Garten des Restaurants sowie der Süßwasserpool. Ein Bad im kristallklaren Salzwasser bietet die private, herrlich italienische Felsenbucht mit Bar und Restaurant, in der das Meer glitzert – silbrig selbstverständlich.

Buchtipp: »Der Graf von Monte Christo« von Alexandre Dumas.

Surplombant la Côte d'Argent

L'origine du nom Monte Argentario, le mont argenté, est un sujet discuté avec passion par les habitants de la région. Certains soutiennent la thèse lumineuse selon laquelle il dériverait des reflets argentés des jeux de lumière du soleil sur la mer ; d'autres renvoient à l'histoire et à la famille noble des Domitii Ahenobarbi, qui soutinrent la République romaine en tant que prêteurs (« argentarii ») et qui reçurent cette région en contrepartie. Toutefois, les deux parties s'accordent pour dire que le Monte Argentario est l'une des plus belles destinations de la Maremme. Au sommet des falaises les plus spectaculaires de ce qui était autrefois une île aujourd'hui reliée à la botte par trois isthmes, se dressent de nombreuses villas appartenant à la jet-set. Toutefois, il n'est pas nécessaire d'être célèbre pour résider en cet endroit sélect : l'hôtel Torre di Cala Piccola, perché à 100 mètres au-dessus de la mer et à quelques kilomètres seulement de Porto Santo Stefano, offre une situation privilégiée. Il est constitué de plusieurs maisons en pierre et en bois qui entourent une tour de guet espagnole en ruine. Renonçant au luxe opulent, les chambres préservent le charme rustique de la région. Les pièces les plus convoitées sont celles donnant sur les îles Giglio, Giannutri et Montecristo ; ce superbe panorama s'étend également sous vos yeux du jardin du restaurant et de la piscine à eau douce. Un bain dans une eau cristalline et salée est possible dans la magnifique baie privée de l'hôtel dotée d'un bar et d'un restaurant. Là aussi, la mer jette des reflets – d'argent cela va de soi.

Livre à emporter : « Le comte de Monte-Cristo » d'Alexandre Dumas.

ANREISE	8 km von Porto Santo Stefano entfernt. Die Distanz zum Flughafen Rom beträgt 145 km.
PREISE	€€
ZIMMER	50 Zimmer.
KÜCHE	Das Restaurant hat sich auf Meeresfrüchte spezialisiert.
GESCHICHTE	Der spanische Wachturm stammt aus dem 17. Jahrhundert. Im rund 30 Jahre alten Hotel werden regelmäßig Teilrenovierungen durchgeführt, zuletzt Anfang 2009.
X-FAKTOR	Eine gute Adresse für Hobbyhistoriker: In der Nähe befinden sich viele etruskische Ausgrabungsstätten.

ACCÈS	À 8 km de Porto Santo Stefano. L'aéroport de Rome est à 145 km.
PRIX	€€
CHAMBRES	50 chambres.
RESTAURATION	Spécialités de fruits de mer.
HISTOIRE	La tour de guet espagnole date du XVIIe siècle. Des travaux de restauration sont régulièrement entrepris dans cet hôtel construit il y a 30 ans, les derniers ont été achevés au début de 2009.
LES « PLUS »	Une bonne adresse pour les passionnés d'histoire. De nombreux sites étrusques se trouvent à proximité.

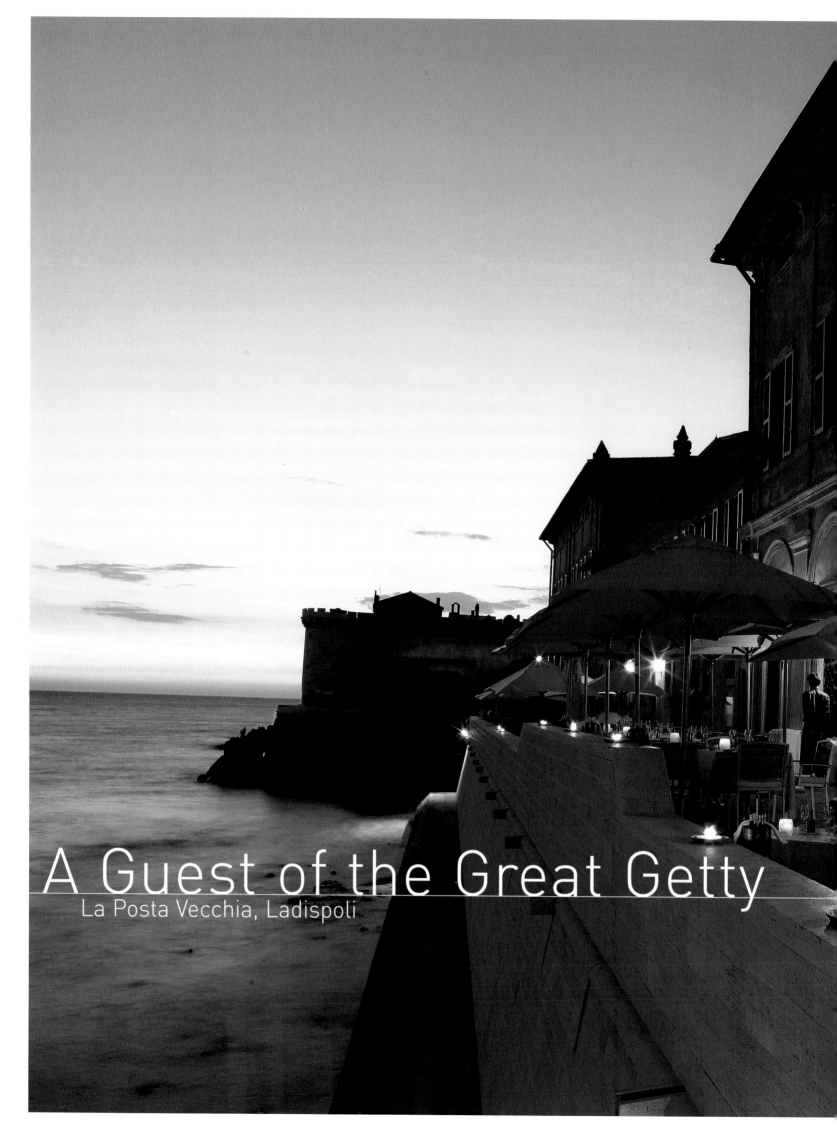

A Guest of the Great Getty

La Posta Vecchia, Ladispoli

La Posta Vecchia, Ladispoli

A Guest of the Great Getty

He loved treasures – oil, which he tracked down under the earth, art, which he collected all over the world, women, who he seduced in his houses. He was hyper, curious and immoderate, and according to his critics was as neurotic as he was wealthy: Jean Paul Getty (1892–1976) was to his dying day the world's richest man, a tycoon and one of the most enigmatic characters of last century. During a trip to Italy he discovered on the coast of Latium an ancient villa that had once served as a guest house for the aristocratic Orsini family and as a post house – he bought the property in 1960 and transformed it into that which an American billionaire imagined a villa of the Old World should be. For the palatial rooms he chose furniture owned by the Medici, French Gobelin tapestries, Venetian mirrors and oil paintings by European masters – almost every exhibit a unique specimen on a par with any museum piece. Getty closed this treasure chest in 1975; today it is open for business once more and as "La Posta Vecchia" is one of Italy's most eccentric hotels. All rooms are named after famous guests – those wishing to get as close as possible to the former head of the household reserve either the Getty Suite or the Medici Suite next door, in which the great man's lovers once lay in an antique bed and bathed in a pink marble bath. Perhaps because Getty harboured a slight fear of the ocean, the sea view does not play a major role in all the rooms – but the interior wouldn't stand for any competition anyway.

Books to pack: "How to Be Rich" by Jean Paul Getty and "Etruscan Places" by D. H. Lawrence.

La Posta Vecchia
Palo Laziale
00055 Ladispoli
Italy
Tel. +39 06 9949 501
Fax +39 06 9949 507
info@lapostavecchia.com
www.lapostavecchia.com
Open from the beginning of April to mid-November

DIRECTIONS	Located on the coast north of Rome, 19 miles from Fiumicino Airport. There is a narrow beach below the hotel.
RATES	€€€
ROOMS	19 rooms.
FOOD	The "Cesar Restaurant" with a terrace overlooking the sea has one Michelin star and serves Italian cuisine.
HISTORY	The villa was built in 1640; it has been a hotel since 1992; today owned by Relais & Châteaux.
X-FACTOR	Getty discovered the ruins of two Roman villas on the grounds. The finds are displayed in a museum in the cellar of the hotel.

Zu Gast beim großen Getty

Er liebte Schätze – Öl, das er unter der Erde aufspürte, Kunst, die er in aller Welt sammelte, Frauen, die er in seinen Häusern verführte. Er stand unter Strom, war neugierig und maßlos und hatte nach Meinung seiner Kritiker fast ebenso viele Neurosen wie Geld: Jean Paul Getty (1892–1976) war bis zu seinem Tod der reichste Mann der Welt, ein Tycoon und eine der schillerndsten Persönlichkeiten des vergangenen Jahrhunderts. Während einer Italienreise entdeckte er an der Küste Latiums eine antike Villa, die einst als Gästehaus der Adelsfamilie Orsini und als Poststation gedient hatte – er kaufte das Anwesen 1960 und verwandelte es in das, was sich ein amerikanischer Milliardär unter einer Villa der alten Welt vorstellte. Für die palastartigen Räume wählte er Möbel aus dem Besitz der Medici, französische Gobelins, venezianische Spiegel und Ölbilder europäischer Meister – so gut wie jedes Exponat ein Unikat mit Museumsqualitäten. Getty schloss diese Schatztruhe 1975; heute ist sie wieder geöffnet und als »La Posta Vecchia« eines der exzentrischsten Hotels Italiens. Alle Zimmer sind nach berühmten Gästen benannt – wer dem ehemaligen Hausherren so nahe wie möglich kommen will, reserviert die Getty-Suite oder die Medici-Suite nebenan, in der seine Geliebten in einem antiken Bett lagen und in einer pinkfarbenen Marmorwanne badeten. Vielleicht weil Getty die See nie ganz geheuer war, spielt Meerblick nicht in allen Räumen die Hauptrolle – doch das Interieur vertrüge ohnehin keine Konkurrenz.

Buchtipps: »Wie wird man reich« von Jean Paul Getty und »Etruskische Orte« von D. H. Lawrence.

Chez le grand Getty

Il aimait les trésors : l'or noir, les œuvres d'art qu'il collectionnait et les femmes qu'il séduisait dans ses demeures. Il était survolté, curieux, excessif et avait selon ses critiques presque autant de névroses que d'argent : Jean Paul Getty (1892-1976) fut jusqu'à sa mort l'homme le plus riche du monde, un magnat du pétrole et l'une des personnalités les plus brillantes du XXᵉ siècle. Lors d'un voyage en Italie, il découvrit sur la côte de la mer Tyrrhénienne une villa ancienne qui avait jadis appartenu à la famille des princes Orsini avant de servir d'hôtel et de relais de poste. Il acheta la propriété en 1960 et la transforma en une villa du Vieux Monde telle que l'imagine un milliardaire américain. Pour les pièces les plus majestueuses, il choisit des meubles ayant appartenu aux Médicis, des tapisseries françaises, des miroirs vénitiens et des tableaux de grands maîtres européens : presque tous les objets exposés étaient uniques et auraient pu figurer dans des musées. Getty a fermé la malle aux trésors en 1975 ; de nos jours, elle est rouverte sous le nom de « La Posta Vecchia », et est l'un des hôtels les plus excentriques d'Italie. Toutes les chambres portent le nom de clients célèbres. Si vous désirez vous faire une idée de la personnalité de l'ancien propriétaire, réservez la suite Getty ou la suite Médicis voisine où ses maîtresses reposaient dans un lit ancien ou prenaient un bain dans une baignoire de marbre rose. Toutes les pièces ne donnent pas sur la mer, peut-être parce que Getty éprouvait envers celle-ci une certaine appréhension, et que leur beauté ne supporterait pas d'être mise en concurrence.

Livres à emporter : « Comment devenir riche » de Jean Paul Getty et « Promenades étrusques » de D. H. Lawrence.

ANREISE	An der Küste nördlich von Rom gelegen, 30 km vom Flughafen Fiumicino entfernt. Unterhalb des Hotels befindet sich ein schmaler Strand.
PREISE	€€€
ZIMMER	19 Zimmer.
KÜCHE	Das »Cesar Restaurant« mit Terrasse zum Meer hat einen Michelin-Stern und serviert italienische Menüs.
GESCHICHTE	Erbaut wurde die Villa 1640, seit 1992 ist sie ein Hotel; heute bei Relais & Châteaux.
X-FAKTOR	Getty entdeckte auf dem Grundstück die Ruinen zweier römischer Villen. Die Fundstücke zeigt ein Museum im Keller des Hauses.

ACCÈS	Sur la côte au nord de Rome, à 30 km de l'aéroport de Fiumicino. Une plage étroite se trouve sous l'hôtel.
PRIX	€€€
CHAMBRES	19 chambres.
RESTAURATION	Le « Cesar Restaurant », avec terrasse sur la mer, a une étoile Michelin et sert une cuisine italienne raffinée.
HISTOIRE	Construite en 1640, la villa est devenue un hôtel en 1992 ; actuellement Relais & Châteaux.
LES « PLUS »	Getty a découvert sur la propriété deux villas romaines. Les vestiges sont visibles dans un musée, dans la cave de la maison.

A Panoramic Place
La Minervetta, Sorrento

La Minervetta, Sorrento

A Panoramic Place

When Don Giovanni Cacace opened the Ristorante La Minervetta in the 1950s, he created a stage for little Italian scenes like those in the movies – with tables on which home-made Mediterranean delicacies were served, a veranda that looked out across the Bay of Naples all the way to Vesuvius, and guests who seemed as vivacious as they did contented. No wonder that even Hollywood stars came here when they were on the coast for shooting or for the Sorrento Film Festival. The glitz and the glamour faded, however, after Don's death, and the building was sold and became a run-of-the-mill accommodation – until Marco De Luca, set designer, interior decorator and Cacace's grandson, intervened. He transformed the building, balanced high on the tuff cliffs, into a modern Mediterranean villa. The rooms are lent a certain loft atmosphere by high glass façades and maintained in glowing red, orange, blue and turquoise tones, with Vietri tiles and collectible figures creating a retro ambience that combines artfulness and kitsch in exactly the right measure. Pictures with maritime echoes pay tribute to the Mediterranean, while the large table in the kitchen, which is accessible to the guests, recalls the grandfather's local bar and every morning serves a delicious, buffet-style breakfast with cappuccino, fresh fruit and pastries. The perfect panorama can be enjoyed from both the terrace and the pool – just like it was back in the fifties; just like it is in film.
Book to pack: "Pictures from Italy" by Charles Dickens.

La Minervetta
Via Capo 25
80067 Sorrento
Italy
Tel. +39 081 877 4455
Fax +39 081 878 4601
info@laminervetta.com
www.laminervetta.com
**Open from the beginning
of April to mid-October**

DIRECTIONS	Situated above the fishing village of Marina Grande. Naples Airport is 32 miles away.
RATES	€€€
ROOMS	11 rooms and 1 suite, all with sea view.
FOOD	A hot breakfast can be ordered. In the evening, guests eat in one of the restaurants at the harbour, which can be reached via a private flight of steps.
HISTORY	Opened 2005.
X-FACTOR	The hotel has no beach, but it does have a splendid sun terrace, covered in plants, 65 feet above the sea, with a view of the fishing boats.

Ein Panoramaplatz

Als Don Giovanni Cacace in den 1950ern das Ristorante
La Minervetta eröffnete, schuf er eine Bühne für italienische
Momente wie im Film – mit Tafeln, an denen hausgemachte
mediterrane Köstlichkeiten serviert wurden, einer Veranda,
die über die Bucht von Neapel bis zum Vesuv blickte, und
Gästen, die ebenso temperamentvoll wie glücklich schienen.
Kein Wunder, dass hierher sogar Hollywoodstars kamen,
wenn sie zu Dreharbeiten oder beim Filmfestival von Sorrent
an der Küste waren. Glanz und Glamour verblassten nach
dem Tod des Don jedoch, das Gebäude wurde verkauft und
zu einer x-beliebigen Herberge – bis Marco De Luca, Bühnen-
bildner, Innenausstatter und Enkel Cacaces, eingriff. Er verwandelte den Bau, der hoch oben an den Tuffsteinfelsen
balanciert, in eine moderne mediterrane Villa. Mit Zimmern,
denen raumhohe Fensterfronten Loft-Flair verleihen, die in
leuchtenden Rot-, Orange-, Blau- und Türkistönen gehalten
sind und in denen Vietri-Fliesen und Sammlerfiguren ein
Retro-Ambiente schaffen, das im genau richtigen Maß
kunstvoll und kitschig ist. Bilder mit maritimen Anklängen
sind eine Hommage ans Mittelmeer, der große Tisch in der
den Gästen zugänglichen Küche erinnert ans Lokal des
Großvaters und dient jeden Morgen als Buffet für ein köst-
liches Frühstück mit Cappuccino, frischen Früchten und
Gebäck. Und von den Terrassen sowie vom Pool genießt
man wieder das perfekte Panorama – wie damals in den
1950ern und wie im Film.
Buchtipp: »Bilder aus Italien« von Charles Dickens.

Une vue panoramique

Quand Don Giovanni Cacace a ouvert le Ristorante La
Minervetta dans les années 1950, il a créé un décor de cinéma pour des tranches de vie italiennes – avec de grandes
tables garnies de délicieux plats méditerranéens faits maison,
une véranda avec vue sur le golfe de Naples jusqu'au Vésuve
et des clients qui semblaient aussi expansifs qu'heureux.
Rien d'étonnant à ce que même des stars d'Hollywood aient
fait le déplacement quand elles étaient en tournage sur la
côte ou au festival de Sorrente. Mais à la mort du Don, tout
le charme a peu à peu disparu, le bâtiment a été vendu et est
devenu une auberge banale jusqu'à ce que Marco De Luca,
scénographe, décorateur et petit-fils de Cacace, entre en
action. Il a transformé cette construction, établie en hauteur
et accrochée aux rochers de tuf, en une villa méditerranéenne
moderne. Les chambres auxquelles de vastes baies vitrées
donnent des allures de loft sont aménagées dans des tons
lumineux de rouge, orange, bleu et turquoise. Elles affichent
toutes un air rétro avec leur carrelage Vietri et leurs objets
de collection, choisis avec goût mais avec une touche de
kitsch. Les tableaux aux réminiscences maritimes sont un
hommage à la Méditerranée, la grande table de la cuisine
ouverte aux clients rappelle le Ristorante du grand-père et le
buffet du délicieux petit déjeuner y est servi avec capuccino,
fruits frais et gâteaux secs. Et depuis les terrasses ainsi que
de la piscine, on jouit d'un panorama de rêve : comme dans
les années 1950 , on se croirait dans un film.
Livre à emporter : « Images d'Italie » de Charles Dickens.

ANREISE	Über dem Fischerdorf Marina Grande gelegen. Der Flug-hafen Neapel ist 52 km entfernt.
PREISE	€€€
ZIMMER	11 Zimmer und 1 Suite; alle mit Meerblick.
KÜCHE	Zum Frühstück können warme Gerichte bestellt werden. Abends isst man in einem der Restaurants am Hafen, zu dem eine private Treppe führt.
GESCHICHTE	2005 eröffnet.
X-FAKTOR	Das Hotel hat keinen Strand, dafür aber eine herrlich eingewachsene Sonnenterrasse 20 m über dem Meer, mit Blick auf die Fischerboote.

ACCÈS	Au-dessus du village de pêcheurs Marina Grande. L'aéroport de Naples est à 52 km.
PRIX	€€€
CHAMBRES	11 chambres et 1 suite ; toutes avec vue sur la mer.
RESTAURATION	Possibilité de commander des plats chauds au petit déjeuner. Le dîner se prend dans l'un des restaurants du port auquel on accède par un escalier privé.
HISTOIRE	Ouvert en 2005.
LES « PLUS »	L'hôtel n'a pas de plage mais une magnifique terrasse à 20 m au-dessus de la mer avec vue sur les bateaux des pêcheurs.

Into the Blue
Grand Hotel Parco dei Principi, Sorrento

Grand Hotel Parco dei Principi, Sorrento

Into the Blue

When the Neapolitan engineer and hotelier Roberto Fernandes engaged the architect Gio Ponti to erect this building at the beginning of the 1960s, he commissioned one of the world's first design hotels. And to this day the Parco dei Principi has remained one of the few design hotels in the world that really deserve the title – it proves how perfectly nature and architecture go together, how timelessly interiors can be presented and how important details can be. Gio Ponti erected the building on the tuff cliffs on the Gulf of Naples and designed it as a complete symphony in blue. The fresh hues of the sky and the sea are repeatedly combined with white and light oak throughout the entire hotel – Ponti's total work of art includes the furnishings and pictures, linen and crockery, even telephones and ashtrays (on the occasion of the hotel's inaugural party the chef, with the wink of an eye, is said to have asked for blue spaghetti). Even during a complete renovation the owners retained the original design in its entirety; this includes the wall panelling of white and blue ceramic tiles as well as the floors laid with majolica tiles, geometric in effect, of which Ponti designed 30 different variations. Though not maintained in blue hues, the 18th-century hotel garden and the private rocky beach are equally worth seeing, the latter being accessed by means of a small lift that descends through the cliffs.
Book to pack: "The Last Days of Pompeii" by Edward Bulwer-Lytton.

Grand Hotel Parco dei Principi	
Via Rota 1	
80067 Sorrento	
Italy	
Tel. +39 081 878 4644	
Fax +39 081 878 3786	
info@hotelparcoprincipi.com	
www.grandhotelparcodeiprincipi.net	
Open all year round	

DIRECTIONS	On the edge of the town of Sorrento. Naples Airport is 31 miles away.
RATES	€€
ROOMS	96 rooms.
FOOD	Mediterranean food is on the menu in the "Ristorante Gio Ponti"; the "Spiaggia" restaurant serves seafood and delicious pizza.
HISTORY	Gio Ponti built the hotel in 1962. Renovation work was carried out true to the original by Fabrizio Mautone and was completed in 2003.
X-FACTOR	The pool, picturesquely concealed in the garden.

Ins Blaue

Als der neapolitanische Ingenieur und Hotelier Roberto Fernandes den Meisterarchitekten Gio Ponti für diesen Bau Anfang der 1960er engagierte, gab er den Auftrag zu einem der ersten Designhotels der Welt. Und bis heute ist das Parco dei Principi eines der wenigen Designhotels, die diesen Titel auch wirklich verdienen – beweist es doch, wie perfekt Natur und Architektur zusammenpassen, wie zeitlos elegant sich Interieurs geben und wie wichtig Details sein können. Gio Ponti hat das Gebäude auf die Tuffstein-felsen am Golf von Neapel gebaut und es ganz als Sinfonie in Blau gestaltet. Die frischen Farbtöne des Himmels und des Meeres finden sich kombiniert mit Weiß und heller Eiche überall wieder – Pontis Gesamtkunstwerk umfasst Mobiliar und Bilder, Leinen und Geschirr, selbst Telefone und Aschenbecher (anlässlich der Eröffnungsparty soll er den Küchenchef mit einem Augenzwinkern sogar um blaue Spaghetti gebeten haben). Selbst im Rahmen einer Rundum-renovierung haben die Besitzer das originale Design voll-ständig beibehalten; inklusive der Wandverkleidungen aus weißen und blauen Keramikkieseln sowie der geometrisch wirkenden Böden aus Majolika-Fliesen, von denen Ponti 30 verschiedene Varianten entworfen hat. Nicht in Blau ge-halten, aber ebenso sehenswert sind der Hotelgarten aus dem 18. Jahrhundert sowie der private Felsenstrand, zu dem ein kleiner Aufzug durch den Felsen hinunterfährt.
Buchtipp: »Die letzten Tage von Pompeji« von Edward Bulwer-Lytton.

Une palette de bleus

Quand Roberto Fernandes, ingénieur et hôtelier napolitain, a engagé au début des années 1960 le célèbre architecte Gio Ponti, il l'a chargé de concevoir l'un des premiers hôtels design au monde. Et de nos jours, le Parco dei Principi est toujours l'un des rares hôtels au monde à vraiment mériter ce titre. Il illustre une parfaite harmonie entre nature et architecture, témoigne d'une élégance intemporelle des intérieurs et de l'importance des détails. Gio Ponti a érigé cet édifice sur une falaise de tuf dominant le golfe de Naples et a créé un décor harmonieux dans une symphonie de bleus. Les fraîches nuances du ciel et de la mer se retrouvent dans tout l'ensemble, combinées à des nuances de blanc et de chêne clair. L'œuvre d'art totale de Ponti englobe le mobilier et les tableaux, les tissus et la vaisselle, jusqu'aux téléphones et cendriers (à l'occasion de l'inauguration, il aurait même demandé au cuisinier en chef d'un air entendu de préparer des spaghettis bleus). Les actuels propriétaires ont soigneu-sement restauré l'hôtel et conservé tout le design d'origine, y compris les revêtements muraux en tesselles de céramique bleue et blanche et les sols carrelés en majolique réalisés par Ponti dans des motifs géométriques en trente versions différentes. Dans d'autres teintes mais également remar-quables : le jardin de l'hôtel qui date du XVIIIe siècle ainsi que la plage privée au pied de la falaise accessible par un petit ascenseur.
Livre à emporter : « Les derniers jours de Pompéi » d'Edward Bulwer-Lytton.

ANREISE	Am Stadtrand von Sorrent gelegen. Der Flughafen Neapel ist 50 km entfernt.
PREISE	€€
ZIMMER	96 Zimmer.
KÜCHE	Im »Ristorante Gio Ponti« stehen mediterrane Menüs auf der Karte, das Restaurant »Spiaggia« serviert Seafood und köstliche Pizza.
GESCHICHTE	Gio Ponti baute das Hotel 1962. Eine originalgetreue Renovierung durch Fabrizio Mautone wurde 2003 abge-schlossen.
X-FAKTOR	Der Pool, der sich malerisch im Garten verbirgt.

ACCÈS	Au bord de la ville de Sorrente. L'aéroport de Naples est à 50 km.
PRIX	€€
CHAMBRES	96 chambres.
RESTAURATION	Le « Ristorante Gio Ponti » propose des menus médi-terranéens, le restaurant « Spiaggia » sert des fruits de mer et de délicieuses pizzas.
HISTOIRE	Gio Ponti a construit l'hôtel en 1962. Une restauration fidèle à l'original a été entreprise par Fabrizio Mautone et achevée en 2003.
LES « PLUS »	La piscine, cachée pittoresquement dans le jardin.

Where the Lemons Grow

Bellevue Syrene, Sorrento

Bellevue Syrene, Sorrento

Where the Lemons Grow

Whether the first Limoncello was produced by fishermen at the beginning of the 20th century as a source of inner warmth or created in a monastery as an elixir of the monks, or whether an Italian nun simply stirred the mixture together in her kitchen, remains unknown, as does the place where the first glass of the legendary lemon liqueur was imbibed in Capri, Amalfi or Sorrento. But the Sorrentians do not dwell for long on such historical details – after all, they know that today the best types of Limoncello come from their town. The citrus plantations are among the treasures and sights of Sorrento, and are almost as famous as the town's dark tuff cliffs and the breathtaking view it affords of Vesuvius. The best panoramic view across the land where the lemons thrive is offered by the Bellevue Syrene, which stands enthroned directly on the coast above the picturesque old town. In former times a villa of the Roman emperor Augustus stood here, later the summer residence of the Counts of Mastrobuono and a hotel in which illustrious guests such as Bavaria's fairy-tale king Ludwig II stayed. Busts and mirrors with a breath of antiquity as well as chandeliers and stucco skirting boards recall the history and are at the same time combined with modern furniture and colours – the pastel tones of the walls in turquoise-blue, pale green or lilac are perfectly mixed. Wonderfully, all rooms in the Bellevue Syrene have their own balcony with a sea view – and those who want to be truly authentic enjoy the postcard panorama along with a glass of Limoncello.

Book to pack: "Coup de Grâce" by Marguerite Yourcenar. (She wrote the book while staying in the hotel in 1938).

Bellevue Syrene
Piazza della Vittoria 5
80067 Sorrento
Italy
Tel. +39 081 8781 024
Fax +39 081 8783 963
info@bellevue.it
www.bellevue.it
Open all year round

DIRECTIONS	33 miles south of Naples Airport.
RATES	€€€
ROOMS	50 rooms, all with sea view.
FOOD	In summer Mediterranean dishes can be enjoyed on the terraces of the "La Pergola" and "Il Pino" restaurants; in winter the indoor establishments "Il Don Giovanni" and "Gli Archi" are open.
HISTORY	The main building dates from the year 1750 and has been a hotel since 1820. It was last renovated in winter 2008/2009.
X-FACTOR	The private rocky beach with sun deck.

Im Land, wo die Zitronen blühn

Ob der erste Limoncello Anfang des 20. Jahrhunderts von Fischern als innerer Wärmequell gebraut wurde, ob er in einem Kloster als Elixier der Mönche entstand oder ihn einfach eine italienische Nonna in ihrer Küche zusammen-rührte: Man weiß es nicht – ebenso wenig, ob das erste Glas des legendären Zitronenlikörs auf Capri, in Amalfi oder in Sorrent getrunken wurde. Doch mit solchen historischen Details halten sich die Sorrentiner nicht lange auf – wissen sie doch, dass die heute besten Limoncello-Sorten aus ihrem Städtchen stammen. Die Zitrusplantagen gehören zu den Schätzen und Sehenswürdigkeiten von Sorrent, sie sind fast ebenso berühmt wie die dunklen Tuffsteinfelsen, auf denen der Ort erbaut wurde, und die atemberaubende Sicht auf den Vesuv, die er eröffnet. Den besten Blick über das Land, wo die Zitronen blühn, bietet das Bellevue Syrene, das direkt an der Küste der pittoresken Altstadt thront. Früher stand an dieser Stelle eine Villa des römischen Kaisers Augustus, später die Sommerresidenz der Grafen Mastrobuono und ein Hotel, in dem illustre Gäste wie Bayerns Märchenkönig Ludwig II. residierten. Antik angehauchte Büsten und Spiegel, Kronleuchter und Stuckleisten erinnern an die Geschichte und werden zugleich mit modernen Möbeln und Farben kombiniert – die Pastelltöne der Wände in Türkisblau, Lindgrün oder Flieder sind einfach perfekt gemischt. Wunderbarerweise besitzen alle Zimmer des Bellevue Syrene einen eigenen Balkon mit Meerblick, auf dem man das Postkartenpanorama genießen kann – ganz stilgetreu bei einem Glas Limoncello.

Buchtipp: »Der Fangschuss« von Marguerite Yourcenar. (Sie schrieb das Buch während ihres Aufenthalts im Hotel 1938.)

Le pays où fleurit le citronnier

On ne connaît pas précisément l'origine du Limoncello : a-t-il été concocté au début du XXe siècle par des pêcheurs qui cherchait à se réchauffer, s'agit-il d'un élixir provenant d'un monastère ou est-il tout simplement né dans la cuisine d'une nonna (grand-mère) italienne... Cela reste un mystère, tout comme de savoir où a été bu le premier verre de cette légendaire liqueur de citron : à Capri, Amalfi ou Sorrente ? Mais les habitants de Sorrente ne se soucient guère de tels détails historiques car ils savent que les meilleures sortes de Limoncello proviennent de leur petite ville. Les citronneraies font partie des trésors et des curiosités de Sorrente, elles sont presque aussi fameuses que les roches tufières sur laquelle la ville est construite et que la vue exceptionnelle qu'elle offre sur le Vésuve. Le Bellevue Syrene, qui trône sur le promontoire de la vieille ville pittoresque de Sorrente, a le plus beau panorama sur les citronniers en fleurs. A cet endroit se dressait une villa romaine de l'empereur Auguste, plus tard la résidence d'été du comte Mastrobuono puis un hôtel, dans lequel d'illustres personnalités ont séjourné comme le roi Louis II de Bavière. Des bustes de style antique et des miroirs, des lustres et des plinthes en stuc rappellent l'histoire des lieux et sont combinés avec des meubles et des couleurs modernes : les tons pastel des murs turquoise, vert tilleul ou lilas s'harmonisent parfaitement. Toutes les chambres du Bellevue Syrene possèdent miraculeusement un balcon avec vue sur la mer où il est possible de jouir du panorama tout en sirotant un verre de Limoncello.

Livre à emporter : « Le coup de grâce » de Marguerite Yourcenar. (Livre écrit pendant son séjour à l'hôtel en 1938).

ANREISE	53 km südlich vom Flughafen Neapel entfernt.	ACCÈS	À 53 km au sud de l'aéroport de Naples.
PREISE	€€€	PRIX	€€€
ZIMMER	50 Zimmer, alle mit Meerblick.	CHAMBRES	50 chambres, toutes avec vue sur la mer.
KÜCHE	Im Sommer genießt man mediterrane Menüs auf den Terrassen der Restaurants »La Pergola« und »Il Pino«; im Winter sind die Innenlokale »Il Don Giovanni« und »Gli Archi« geöffnet.	RESTAURATION	En été, une cuisine méditerranéenne est servie en terrasse des restaurants « La Pergola » et « Il Pino » ; « Il Don Giovanni » et « Gli Archi » sont ouverts pendant les mois d'hiver.
GESCHICHTE	Das Hauptgebäude stammt aus dem Jahr 1750 und ist seit 1820 ein Hotel. Im Winter 2008/2009 wurde das Haus zuletzt renoviert.	HISTOIRE	Le bâtiment principal date de 1750 et est devenu un hôtel en 1820. La villa a été rénovée durant l'hiver 2008/2009.
X-FAKTOR	Der private Felsenstrand mit Sonnendeck.	LES « PLUS »	La plage-plateforme privée avec transats et parasols.

A Rich Heritage
Villa Krupp, Capri

Villa Krupp, Capri

Open from April to October

A Rich Heritage

If Villa Krupp had already borne the name of the German industrialist Friedrich Alfred Krupp in 1908, one of its most famous guests would presumably never have stayed here: in that year Lenin visited Maxim Gorki, who lived in the villa in exile – a photo in the visitors' book shows Lenin playing a game of chess on the terrace. But back then the place was harmlessly called Villa Blaesus; only later was it named after the steel magnate. The great man had never lived here himself, but he had commissioned the blasting of the Via Krupp out of the rock. The road snakes in hairpin bends down to Marina Piccola, where Krupp's ship lay anchored. And it is this almost dizzying scenery that the sensational view from the rooms on the top floor takes in; furthermore, the rooms point directly towards Capri's emblem, the Faraglioni rocks. The fact that guests sit on rickety plastic or metal chairs while gazing in wonder across this postcard idyll does not disturb – rather this is one of the details that contribute to the charm of the villa. Straight out of an Italian textbook, the guest house is run as warm-heartedly as it is resolutely by the women of the Coppola family, possesses plain and simple rooms with tiled floors and antiques as well as a pinch of kitsch, and limits its offer of food to breakfast. This, however, is served on the terrace – and you can only hope that Lenin looked up from the chessboard, at least for a moment. Because only then could he have taken more from Capri home with him than a mere checkmate.

Books to pack: "Mother" by Maxim Gorki, written in the Villa Blaesus of the time, and "The Skin" by Curzio Malaparte.

Villa Krupp
Viale Matteotti 12
80073 Capri
Italy
Tel. +39 081 837 0362 and +39 081 837 7473
Fax +39 081 837 6489
villakrupp.dona@alice.it
www.villakrupp.it
Open from April to October

DIRECTIONS	Capri lies 45 to 75 min away from Naples by ship (depending on the type of ferry). From the harbour a funicular and taxis go to the piazzetta, and from there it is a 10 min walk to Villa Krupp.
RATES	€
ROOMS	12 rooms.
FOOD	The owners give good tips for restaurants in which to have lunch and dinner.
HISTORY	The villa was built in 1900 and last renovated in 2007.
X-FACTOR	Marina Piccola is a wonderful place for a dip. If the Via Krupp to the bay is closed, buses and taxis go there from Piazzetta Martiri d'Ungheria.

Ein reiches Erbe

Hätte die Villa Krupp 1908 schon den Namen des deutschen Industriellen Friedrich Alfred Krupp getragen, wäre einer ihrer berühmtesten Gäste vermutlich niemals hier abgestiegen: Lenin besuchte in diesem Jahr Maxim Gorki, der in der Villa im Exil lebte – ein Foto im Gästebuch zeigt Lenin bei einer Partie Schach auf der Terrasse. Doch damals hieß das Haus noch unverfänglich Villa Blaesus, erst später benannte man es nach dem Stahlmagnaten. Dieser hatte zwar selbst nie hier gewohnt, aber direkt unter dem Gebäude die Via Krupp in den Fels schlagen lassen. Die Straße schlängelt sich in Haarnadelkurven hinunter zur Marina Piccola, wo Krupps Schiff vor Anker lag. Auf diese fast schwindelerregende Szenerie eröffnen die Zimmer im Obergeschoss einen sensationellen Blick; sie zeigen zudem direkt auf Capris Wahrzeichen, die Faraglioni-Felsen. Dass man beim Bestaunen dieser Postkartenidylle auf wackligen Plastik- oder Metallstühlen sitzt, stört nicht – vielmehr ist dies eines der Details, die den Charme der Villa ausmachen. Die Pension wie aus dem Italien-Lehrbuch wird von den Frauen der Familie Coppola so herzlich wie resolut geführt, besitzt schlichte Zimmer mit Fliesenböden, Antiquitäten sowie einer Prise Kitsch und beschränkt das kulinarische Angebot aufs Frühstück. Dieses jedoch wird auf der Aussichtsterrasse serviert – und man hofft sehr, dass Lenin damals zumindest kurz die Augen vom Spielbrett gehoben hat. Denn nur dann konnte er mehr von Capri mit nach Hause nehmen als ein »Schachmatt«.

Buchtipps: »Die Mutter« von Maxim Gorki, das er in der damaligen Villa Blaesus schrieb, und »Die Haut« von Curzio Malaparte.

Un riche héritage

Si la Villa Krupp avait déjà porté le nom de l'industriel allemand en 1908, un de ces plus célèbres clients n'y serait probablement jamais descendu. Cette année-là, Lénine rendait visite à Maxime Gorki, l'exilé, qui résidait dans cette villa à Capri : une photo dans le livre d'or témoigne d'une partie d'échecs avec Lénine sur la terrasse. La maison portait jadis le nom encore anodin de villa Blaesus, ce n'est que plus tard qu'elle fut baptisée d'après le nom du magnat de l'acier. Certes, il n'y a jamais vécu lui-même mais il était le constructeur de la Via Krupp, découpée dans les rochers directement sous le bâtiment. Cette route mène avec ses virages en épingle à cheveux à Marina Piccola, en contrebas, où le bateau de Krupp était jadis au mouillage. Dans ce cadre à donner le vertige, les chambres du premier étage de la villa offrent une vue sensationnelle. Elles donnent directement sur l'emblème de Capri : les rochers Faraglioni. Que l'on admire ce paysage de carte postale en étant assis sur des chaises en métal ou en plastique branlantes ne gêne aucunement. Ce détail fait plutôt partie du charme de la villa. Cette pension typiquement italienne est dirigée par les femmes de la famille Coppola avec un vrai sens de la rigueur et de l'hospitalité. Les chambres carrelées sont simples, meublées d'antiquités et un peu kitsch. Le petit déjeuner, seul repas proposé, est servi sur la terrasse panoramique et, devant cette vue grandiose, on espère vraiment que Lénine a, au moins pendant un bref instant, levé les yeux de son échiquier afin de garder en souvenir de Capri plus qu'un « échec et mat ».

Livres à emporter : « La mère » de Maxime Gorki écrit dans l'ancienne Villa Blaesus et « La peau » de Curzio Malaparte.

ANREISE	Capri liegt 45 bis 75 Schiffsminuten vor Neapel (je nach Fährtyp). Vom Hafen fahren Standseilbahn und Taxis zur Piazzetta, von dort aus läuft man 10 min zur Villa Krupp.	ACCÈS	Capri est à 45 voire 75 min en bateau de Naples. Un funiculaire et des taxis mènent du port à la Piazzetta ; la villa Krupp se trouve à 10 min à pied.
PREISE	€	PRIX	€
ZIMMER	12 Zimmer.	CHAMBRES	12 chambres.
KÜCHE	Die Besitzer geben gute Tipps für Restaurants zum Mittag- und Abendessen.	RESTAURATION	Les propriétaires ont de bonnes adresses de restaurants pour le déjeuner et le dîner.
GESCHICHTE	Die 1900 erbaute Villa wurde 2007 zuletzt renoviert.	HISTOIRE	Cette villa construite en 1900 a été rénovée pour la dernière fois en 2007.
X-FAKTOR	An der Marina Piccola kann man wunderbar baden. Ist die Via Krupp zur Bucht geschlossen, fahren ab der Piazzetta Martiri d'Ungheria Busse und Taxis dorthin.	LES « PLUS »	Baignades sublimes à Marina Piccola. Des cars et taxis mènent aussi à la baie à partir de Piazzetta Martiri d'Ungheria.

Days for Dreaming
La Conca del Sogno, Nerano

La Conca del Sogno, Nerano

Days for Dreaming

There are places that remain known only to insiders even when they have achieved a certain reputation – because they are wonderfully remote and make their visitors into discoverers, because their surroundings are so utterly beautiful that they touch the soul, and because they preserve their own charm, independent of all fashions and trends. La Conca del Sogno is such a place: the "Bay of Dreams" lies on a wildly romantic section of the Amalfi Coast – the most beautiful route to which is either on foot or by boat, with crystal-clear water and surrounded by steep cliffs. Once, the Tizzani family ran a quarry here and exported the stone to numerous countries – but at the end of the 1950s the business, arduous enough anyway, became too expensive, and Pietro Tizzani made a long-held dream come true: together with his wife, Giuseppina, he opened a small restaurant, whose speciality was fresh fish. Today La Conca del Sogno is run by the Tizzanis' children and is still famous for its delicious seafood (the menu is best put together by the owners, who possess an infallible feel for the culinary preferences of each individual guest). From the terrace, you look out to the Galli Islands; this panoramic view is offered by most of the rooms on the top floor, which are simply furnished and in the colours of the sun, sea and sky. It is not possible to find a quieter place than here to dream your way through the day – La Conca del Sogno lives up to its name in every way.

Book to pack: "Italian Journey" by Johann Wolfgang von Goethe.

La Conca del Sogno
Via San Marciano 9
80061 Nerano
Italy
Tel. +39 081 808 1036
info@concadelsogno.it
www.concadelsogno.it
Open all year round

DIRECTIONS	Guests are picked up by boat in Marina del Cantone. Those who come by car should follow the signs to "Nerano" and "Camping Sirenuse" from Massa Lubrense and continue on to the bay at the end of the road.
RATES	€
ROOMS	9 rooms.
FOOD	Good wines are expertly recommended to accompany the Mediterranean meals.
HISTORY	The Tizzanis have run the restaurant since 1992.
X-FACTOR	The catch of the day is presented in basins below the restaurant.

Traumhafte Tage

Es gibt Orte, die Geheimtipps bleiben, selbst wenn sie ein gewisses Renommee erreicht haben – weil sie wunderbar abgelegen sind und ihre Besucher zugleich zu Entdeckern machen, weil ihre Umgebung so vollkommen schön ist, dass sie die Seele berührt, und weil sie unabhängig von allen Moden und Trends ihren eigenen Charme behalten. La Conca del Sogno ist solch ein Ort: Die »Bucht der Träume« liegt an einem wildromantischen Abschnitt der Amalfiküste – am schönsten zu Fuß oder per Boot erreichbar, mit kristallklarem Wasser und eingerahmt von schroffen Felsen. Einst betrieb die Familie Tizzani hier einen Steinbruch und exportierte den Fels in zahlreiche Länder – doch Ende der 1950er-Jahre wurde das ohnehin mühsame Geschäft zu teuer, und Pietro Tizzani erfüllte sich einen lang ersehnten Wunsch: Gemeinsam mit seiner Frau Giuseppina eröffnete er ein kleines Restaurant, dessen größte Spezialität frischer Fisch war. Heute wird La Conca del Sogno von den Kindern der Tizzanis geführt und ist noch immer für seine köstlichen Meeresfrüchte berühmt (das Menü lässt man sich am besten von den Besitzern zusammenstellen, die ein untrügliches Gespür für die kulinarischen Vorlieben jedes einzelnen Gastes haben). Von der Terrasse aus fällt der Blick auf die drei Galli-Inseln; dieses Panorama eröffnen auch die meisten Zimmer im Obergeschoss, die schlicht und in den Farben von Sonne, Himmel und Meer eingerichtet sind. Ungestörter als hier kann man sich nicht durch den Tag träumen – La Conca del Sogno macht ihrem Namen alle Ehre.

Buchtipp: »Italienische Reise« von Johann Wolfgang von Goethe.

Un séjour de rêve

Il y a des endroits réservés aux initiés, même s'ils ont atteint une certaine renommée, parce qu'ils sont merveilleusement isolés et qu'ils font de leurs visiteurs des explorateurs, parce que leurs paysages sont d'une telle beauté qu'ils nous émeuvent et parce qu'ils conservent leur propre charme indépendamment des modes et tendances. La Conca del Sogno est l'un de ces endroits : la « baie des rêves » est située sur un tronçon sauvage et romantique de la côte almafitaine, entre des eaux cristallines et des rochers escarpés. Pour accéder à ce site de la manière la plus impressionnante qui soit, prenez le bateau ou empruntez le chemin à pied. Vous ne le regretterez pas. Autrefois, la famille Tizzani avait ici une carrière et exportait la roche dans de nombreux pays. A la fin des années 1950, ce commerce pénible devint également trop cher, et Pietro Tizzani réalisa un des ces rêves de jeunesse : il ouvrit avec sa femme Giuseppina un petit restaurant dont la spécialité était le poisson. De nos jours, la Conca del Sogno est dirigée par leurs enfants et est toujours réputée pour ses délicieux fruits de mer (laissez les propriétaires composer votre menu, ils ont un flair inouï pour deviner les préférences culinaires de leurs clients). Depuis la terrasse, vous apercevrez les trois îles Galli. La plupart des chambres à l'étage supérieur jouissent également de ce panorama. Leur décor est simple et dans des tons qui évoquent le soleil, le ciel et la mer. Il n'est pas d'endroit où l'on puisse rêver plus tranquillement : la Conca del Sogno fait vraiment honneur à son nom.

Livre à emporter : « Voyage en Italie » de Johann Wolfgang von Goethe.

ANREISE	Gäste werden mit dem Boot in Marina del Cantone abgeholt. Wer mit dem Auto kommt, folgt ab Massa Lubrense den Schildern »Nerano« und »Camping Sirenuse« und fährt weiter bis zur Bucht am Ende der Straße.
PREISE	€
ZIMMER	9 Zimmer.
KÜCHE	Zu den mediterranen Menüs werden fachkundig gute Weine empfohlen.
GESCHICHTE	Die Geschwister Tizzani leiten das Restaurant seit 1992.
X-FAKTOR	Der Fang des Tages wird in Becken unterhalb des Lokals präsentiert.

ACCÈS	Les clients sont accueillis à Marina del Cantone pour la traversée en bateau. Si vous êtes en voiture, suivre à partir de Massa Lubrense les panneaux « Nerano » et « Camping Sirenuse » puis continuer jusqu'à la baie, au bout de la route.
PRIX	€
CHAMBRES	9 chambres.
RESTAURATION	De très bons vins sont recommandés avec les menus méditerranéens.
HISTOIRE	Les enfants Tizzani gèrent le restaurant depuis 1992.
LES « PLUS »	La pêche du jour est présentée dans des bassins en contrebas.

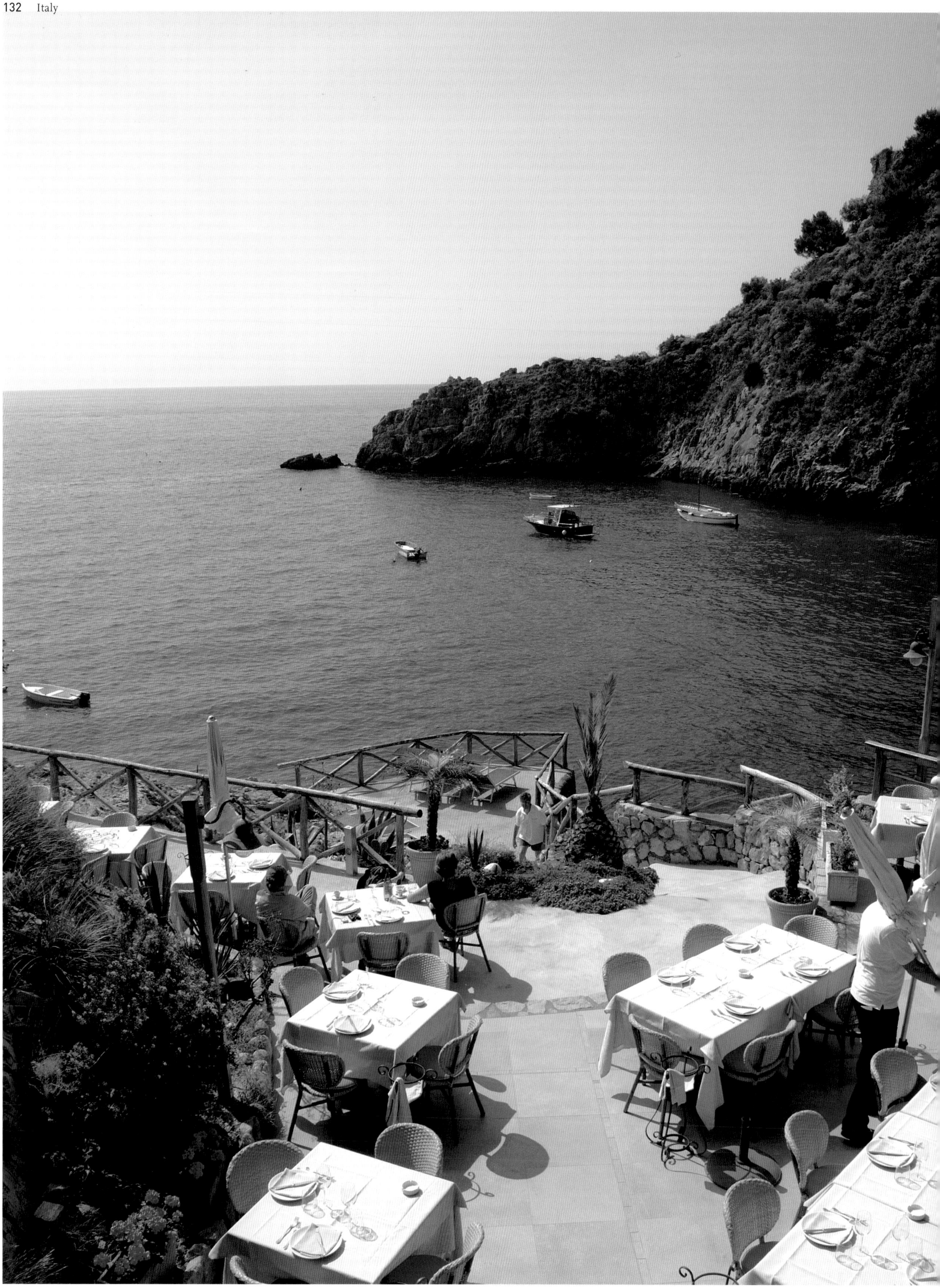

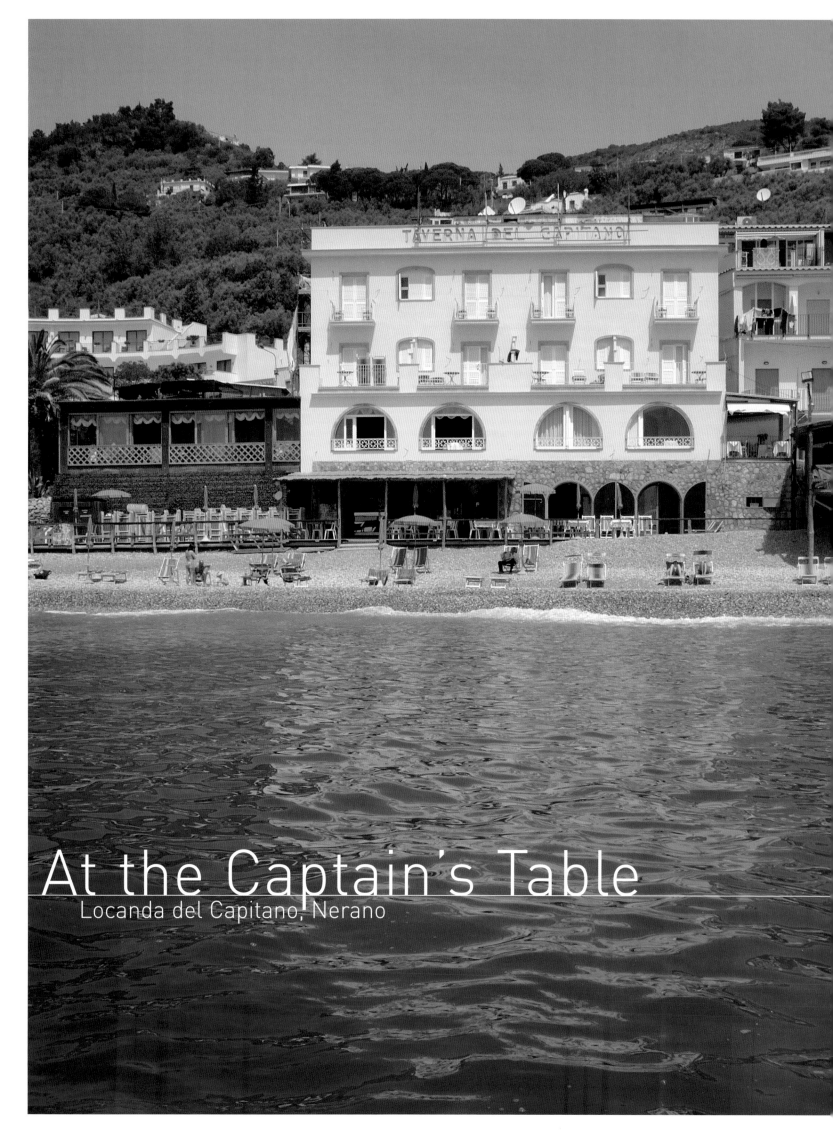

At the Captain's Table
Locanda del Capitano, Nerano

Locanda del Capitano, Nerano

At the Captain's Table

In antiquity the sirens, mythical creatures that with their bewitching singing lured sailors landward and killed them, lived on this coast – Orpheus could resist them only because he sang more sweetly; Odysseus because he had himself tied to the mast of his ship. Today, thankfully, no one must fear for life and limb, indeed the opposite is true. The Taverna del Capitano, in particular, is an establishment at which body and soul can be well and truly spoilt. Standing on the beach of Marina del Cantone, it was created from an old fisherman's house and is owned by the Caputo family, whose members work without exception in the company – led by head cook Alfonso, who takes traditional recipes of the region and gives them a modern interpretation. His seafood antipasti, home-made pasta, finely seasoned fish dishes and desserts to make you melt are beautifully presented and taste so good that even the Michelin Guide's critics were convinced – two stars twinkle above Alfonso's cuisine. Owing to this distinction it is advisable to book (ideally a table at the window with a view across the bay), but diners can then look forward to warm, friendly service and an atmosphere that has remained down to earth. The wine cellar is also award-winning – and those who don't wish to wend their merry way back to the hotel after dinner can spend the night in the pleasantly unpretentious rooms of the Locanda del Capitano on the upper floors and the next morning enjoy a breakfast with delicious-smelling bread, fresh from the oven.

Book to pack: "The Odyssey" by Homer.

Taverna del Capitano (with Locanda del Capitano)	
Piazza delle Sirene 10/11, Località Marina del Cantone	
80061 Massa Lubrense	
Italy	
Tel. +39 081 808 1028	
Fax +39 081 808 1892	
tavdelcap@inwind.it	
www.tavernadelcapitano.it	
Open all year round (restaurant closed on Mondays & Tuesdays; in peak season Mondays only)	

DIRECTIONS	Some 16 miles southwest of Positano, 42 miles south of Naples Airport.
RATES	€€
ROOMS	10 rooms and 2 suites.
FOOD	Just about all the ingredients come from the organic farms of the region.
HISTORY	The Caputos have lived in Nerano for three generations: Alfonso was the most highly thought of man in the village, Salvatore founded the Taverna, today it is run by the young Alfonso.
X-FACTOR	The suites have fantastic terraces with a sea view.

Am Tisch des Kapitäns

In der Antike lebten an dieser Küste die Sirenen: Die Fabelwesen, die mit betörendem Gesang Seefahrer an Land lockten und sie töteten – Orpheus konnte ihnen nur widerstehen, weil er selbst noch süßer sang; Odysseus, weil er sich am Mast seines Schiffes festbinden ließ. Heute muss hier glücklicherweise niemand mehr um Leib und Leben bangen, ganz im Gegenteil. Vor allem die Taverna del Capitano ist eine Adresse, die Körper und Seele rundum verwöhnt. Sie steht am Strand der Marina del Cantone, ist aus einem ehemaligen Fischerhaus entstanden und im Besitz der Familie Caputo. Deren Mitglieder arbeiten ohne Ausnahme im Betrieb – allen voran Chefkoch Alfonso, der traditionelle Rezepte der Region modern interpretiert. Seine Meeresfrüchte-Antipasti, hausgemachten Nudeln, raffiniert gewürzten Fischgerichte und Desserts zum Dahinschmelzen werden wunderschön präsentiert und schmecken so gut, dass selbst die Kritiker des Guide Michelin überzeugt waren – über Alfonsos Küche funkeln zwei Sterne. Aufgrund dieser Auszeichnung sollte man reservieren (am besten einen Tisch am Fenster mit Blick über die Bucht), darf sich dann aber auf ein bodenständig gebliebenes Ambiente und herzlichen Service freuen. Auch der Weinkeller ist preisgekrönt – wer nach einem weinseligen Dinner den Weg ins Hotel nicht mehr antreten möchte, kann in den sympathisch unprätentiösen Zimmern der Locanda del Capitano in den oberen Etagen übernachten und am nächsten Morgen ein Frühstück mit duftendem Brot frisch aus dem Ofen genießen.
Buchtipp: »Die Odyssee« von Homer.

A la table du capitaine

Dans l'Antiquité, cette côte était peuplée de sirènes. Ces créatures mythologiques avaient la réputation de charmer les navigateurs de leur chant et de les attirer sur les récifs afin de les tuer. Orphée put neutraliser leur appel grâce à son chant encore plus harmonieux ; Ulysse, quant à lui, résista en se faisant attacher au mât de son bateau. Heureusement, de nos jours, plus personne ne doit avoir peur pour sa vie dans ce cadre merveilleux, bien au contraire. La Taverna del Capitano est une adresse où l'on nourrit autant le corps que l'esprit. Ancienne maison de pêcheurs, ce restaurant se dresse sur la plage de la Marina del Cantone et appartient à la famille Caputo. Tous les membres de la famille y travaillent sans exception, le plus créatif étant certainement le cuisinier en chef Alfonso, qui modernise les recettes traditionnelles de la région. Ses antipasti de fruits de mer, ses pâtes fraîches maison, ses plats de poisson relevés et raffinés ainsi que ses desserts à se damner sont magnifiquement présentés et si succulents qu'ils ont même convaincu les critiques du guide Michelin : deux étoiles brillent au-dessus de la cuisine d'Alfonso. Par conséquent, il vaut mieux réserver pour être sûr d'avoir une table (si possible près de la fenêtre pour profiter de la vue sur la baie). L'ambiance y est demeurée authentique et le service est empressé. La cave à vins a également été primée et si vous ne voulez pas rejoindre votre hôtel après un dîner bien arrosé, vous pouvez passer la nuit dans une des chambres sympathiques mais sans prétention de la Locanda del Capitano, dans les étages supérieurs. Le lendemain matin, on vous servira au petit déjeuner du pain tout chaud sortant du four.
Livre à emporter : « L'Odyssée » d'Homère.

ANREISE	25 km südwestlich von Positano, 68 km südlich vom Flughafen Neapel gelegen.
PREISE	€€
ZIMMER	10 Zimmer und 2 Suiten.
KÜCHE	So gut wie alle Zutaten stammen aus biologischen Betrieben der Region.
GESCHICHTE	Die Caputos leben seit drei Generationen in Nerano: Alfonso war der am meisten geschätzte Mann im Dorf, Salvatore gründete die Taverna, heute führt sie der junge Alfonso.
X-FAKTOR	Die Suiten besitzen Traumterrassen mit Meerblick.

ACCÈS	À 25 km au sud-ouest de Positano, à 68 km au sud de l'aéroport de Naples.
PRIX	€€
CHAMBRES	10 chambres et 2 suites.
RESTAURATION	Presque tous les ingrédients sont issus de l'agriculture ou de l'élevage biologiques de la région.
HISTOIRE	Les Caputo vivent depuis trois générations à Nerano : Alfonso, le grand-père, était déjà très apprécié dans le village, son fils Salvatore a fondé la Taverna et c'est aujourd'hui le petit-fils Alfonso qui la dirige.
LES « PLUS »	Les suites sont pourvues de terrasses de rêve avec vue sur la mer.

The House of the Mermaids
Le Sirenuse, Positano

Le Sirenuse, Positano

The House of the Mermaids

He had the impression that the world was vertical in Positano – "You do not walk to visit a friend, you either climb or slide," noted American author John Steinbeck in 1953. He visited the little town on the Amalfi Coast at the beginning of the 1950s; when afterwards he wrote an essay for the glossy magazine "Harper's Bazaar", the number of visitors to the place rose to hitherto unknown heights. During his research Steinbeck stayed in Le Sirenuse, the former summer residence of the Marchesi Sersale, which at the time had just been converted into a luxury hotel. Today it is still owned by the family and is run by Antonio Sersale with much love for detail: the mermaid motif that gave the hotel its name appears on key rings, table legs and in frescoes, on the terrace the champagne is served in Murano glasses and the floors of the classic, elegant rooms are fitted with hand-painted tiles. In order to enjoy the loveliest sea view that Positano has to offer, reserve a room on the uppermost floor and insist on a balcony – the higher price will be repaid with every bat of the eyelid. There are, however, two things for which it is worth leaving the panorama to its own devices for a short while: a visit to the spa, designed by Gae Aulenti, and dinner at "La Sponda" – by the light of hundreds of candles.

Book to pack: "The Talented Mr Ripley" by Patricia Highsmith.

Le Sirenuse
Via Cristoforo Colombo 30
84017 Positano
Italy
Tel. +39 089 875 066
Fax +39 089 811 798
info@sirenuse.it
www.sirenuse.it
**Open from mid-March to
the beginning of November**

DIRECTIONS	Le Sirenuse lies in the heart of Positano. Naples Airport is 24 miles away.
RATES	€€€€
ROOMS	63 rooms.
FOOD	"La Sponda" serves fine Neapolitan dishes. The champagne and oyster bar on the terrace is classy.
HISTORY	The palace was built in the 18th century and has been a hotel since 1951. The hotel was renovated in the 1990s.
X-FACTOR	The missing beach is made up for by a pool surrounded by lemon trees.

Das Haus der Meerjungfrauen

In Positano habe er den Eindruck, die Welt stehe senkrecht – und wolle man einen Freund besuchen, laufe man nicht, sondern rolle oder klettere, bemerkte der amerikanische Schriftsteller John Steinbeck 1953. Er besuchte das Städtchen an der Amalfiküste Anfang der 1950er-Jahre und verfasste anschließend einen Essay für das Hochglanzmagazin »Harper's Bazaar«, der die Gästezahlen des Ortes in vorher nie geahnte Höhen steigen ließ. Während seiner Recherchen wohnte Steinbeck im Le Sirenuse, der ehemaligen Sommerresidenz der Marchesi Sersale, die damals gerade in ein Luxushotel umgebaut worden war. Es ist noch heute in Familienbesitz und wird von Antonio Sersale mit viel Liebe zum Detail geführt: Das Motiv der Meerjungfrau, die dem Haus seinen Namen gab, erscheint an Schlüsselanhängern, Tischbeinen und in Wandbildern, auf der Terrasse wird der Champagner in Murano-Gläsern serviert, und die Böden der klassisch-eleganten Zimmer sind mit handbemalten Fliesen ausgelegt. Um den schönsten Meerblick zu genießen, den Positano zu bieten hat, sollte man einen Raum in den obersten Etagen reservieren und unbedingt auf einem Balkon bestehen – den höheren Preis bekommt man mit jedem Wimpernschlag zurückgezahlt. Zwei Gelegenheiten gibt es aber, für die es sich lohnt, das Panorama für einen Moment Panorama sein zu lassen: Einen Besuch im von Gae Aulenti designten Spa und ein Dinner im »La Sponda« – im Schein von Hunderten von Kerzen.

Buchtipp: »Der talentierte Mr. Ripley« von Patricia Highsmith.

Le refuge des sirènes

En 1953, l'écrivain américain John Steinbeck notait qu'il avait l'impression qu'à Positano le monde était à la verticale et que si l'on voulait rendre visite à un ami, on ne devait pas marcher mais rouler ou grimper. Ayant visité cette petite ville de la côte amalfitaine au début des années 1950, il avait ensuite rédigé pour le magazine de renom « Harper's Bazaar » un essai qui connut aussitôt un grand succès et déclencha un véritable engouement pour ce petit village de pêcheurs. Lors de ses recherches, Steinbeck avait séjourné au Sirenuse, l'ancienne résidence d'été du Marchesi Sersale, tout juste transformée à ce moment-là en hôtel de luxe. La famille en est toujours propriétaire et c'est Antonio Sersale qui dirige l'hôtel avec un véritable amour du détail : le motif de la sirène qui a donné son nom à la maison se retrouve sur les porte clés, les pieds de tables et les peintures murales. Le champagne est servi dans des flûtes en verre de Murano et le carrelage des chambres élégantes et classiques est peint à la main. Pour profiter de la plus belle vue de Positano sur la mer, réservez une chambre au dernier étage et insistez pour avoir un balcon. Vous ne regretterez pas l'investissement, le panorama sur les eaux turquoises vous le rendra bien. Toutefois, deux autres points forts de l'hôtel valent de délaisser la vue pour un instant : une visite au spa dessiné par Gae Aulenti et un dîner au restaurant « La Sponda » à la lueur de centaines de bougies.

Livre à emporter : « Le talentueux M. Ripley » de Patricia Highsmith.

ANREISE	Le Sirenuse liegt im Herzen von Positano. Der Flughafen von Neapel ist 55 km entfernt.
PREISE	€€€€
ZIMMER	63 Zimmer.
KÜCHE	»La Sponda« serviert feine neapolitanische Menüs. Stilvoll ist auch die Champagner- und Austernbar auf der Terrasse.
GESCHICHTE	Der Palast stammt aus dem 18. Jahrhundert und ist seit 1951 ein Hotel. In den 1990ern wurde das Haus renoviert.
X-FAKTOR	Den fehlenden Strand ersetzt ein Pool, der von Zitronenbäumen umgeben ist.

ACCÈS	Le Sirenuse se trouve au centre de Positano. L'aéroport de Naples est à 55 km.
PRIX	€€€€
CHAMBRES	63 chambres.
RESTAURATION	« La Sponda » sert une cuisine napolitaine raffinée. Bar à huîtres et à champagne sur la terrasse.
HISTOIRE	Le palais date du XVIIIe siècle et a été transformé en hôtel en 1951. La maison a été rénovée dans les années 1990.
LES « PLUS »	Une piscine entourée de citronniers fait oublier l'absence de plage.

Ravello's Magic Garden
Hotel Caruso, Ravello

Hotel Caruso, Ravello

Ravello's Magic Garden

Almost all geniuses experience creative crises. When Richard Wagner came to Ravello in 1880, he was stuck on the second act of "Parsifal" – until he took a stroll through the park of a villa in Ravello and there found his inspiration for Klingsor's magic garden. Since then, Ravello has competed with Bayreuth as Wagner's town; in 1953 an annual classical music festival, consistently featuring high-ranking performers, was founded in his honour. One of the initiators was Paolo Caruso, whose eponymous luxury hotel was the best establishment in town. And even if the hotel today is no longer owned by the family, it has retained its status – those who come to listen to the stars of the Wagner scene stay here in a manner befitting their station. Housed in an 11th-century palace, the Caruso stands imposingly 1000 feet above the sea – like a loge with a fabulous view of the Amalfi Coast. Those who shy away from investing in a deluxe suite need only to reserve a table on the veranda of the restaurant "Caruso" or to glide across the infinity pool, and they have also hit the jackpot. In the interior the hotel boasts vaulted ceilings and marble floors, Roman columns and 18th-century frescoes – Italian grandezza and allegrezza are perfectly paired here. However, perhaps the most beautiful place in the Caruso is its garden, in which palms and orange trees stand, daisies and hydrangeas bloom and roses garland the "Belvedere" arbour. If Richard Wagner could come to Ravello again today, he would find Klingsor's second magic garden here.

Books to pack: "Lady Chatterley's Lover" by D. H. Lawrence and "The Decameron" by Giovanni Boccaccio.

Hotel Caruso	
Piazza San Giovanni Del Toro 2	
84010 Ravello	
Italy	
Tel. +39 089 858 801	
Fax +39 089 858 806	
info@hotelcaruso.com	
www.hotelcaruso.com	
Open from the beginning of	
April to the end of October	

DIRECTIONS	Naples Airport is 40 miles away.
RATES	€€€€
ROOMS	24 rooms and 24 suites.
FOOD	Along with the Italian restaurant "Caruso" there is the "Belvedere" pool restaurant and two bars.
HISTORY	In 1893 the Caruso family rented out five rooms of the "Pensione Belvedere", from 1903 the house bore the name "Hotel Caruso". In 1999 Orient Express took over the hotel, renovated it and celebrated its reopening in 2005.
X-FACTOR	The visitors' book with dedications from stars like Alexander Fleming, Humphrey Bogart and Jackie Kennedy.

Ravellos Zaubergarten

Fast alle Genies haben Schaffenskrisen. Als Richard Wagner 1880 nach Ravello kam, steckte er im zweiten Akt von »Parsifal« fest – bis er durch den Park einer Villa in Ravello spazierte und dort seine Inspiration für Klingsors Zaubergarten fand. Seitdem macht Ravello Bayreuth als Wagnerstadt Konkurrenz; 1953 wurde sogar ein jährliches und stets hochrangig besetztes Klassikfestival zu seinen Ehren ins Leben gerufen. Zu den Initiatoren zählte Paolo Caruso, der mit dem gleichnamigen Luxushotel die beste Adresse des Ortes führte. Und auch wenn das Haus heute nicht mehr in Familienbesitz ist: Seinen Status hat es behalten – wer den Stars der Wagner-Szene lauschen will, wohnt hier standesgemäß. Untergebracht in einem Palast aus dem 11. Jahrhundert, thront das Caruso 300 Meter hoch über dem Meer – wie eine Loge mit sagenhafter Sicht über die Amalfiküste. Wer die Investition in eine Deluxe Suite scheut, braucht nur einen Tisch auf der Veranda des Restaurants »Caruso« zu reservieren oder in den randlosen Pool zu gleiten und hat ebenfalls das große Los gezogen. Im Inneren besitzt das Hotel Gewölbedecken und Marmorböden, römische Säulen und Fresken aus dem 18. Jahrhundert – italienische Grandezza und Allegrezza bilden hier ein perfektes Paar. Der vielleicht schönste Platz des Caruso aber ist sein Garten, in dem Palmen und Orangenbäume stehen, Margeriten und Hortensien blühen und Rosen den »Belvedere«-Laubengang umkränzen. Könnte Richard Wagner heute nochmals nach Ravello kommen: Hier fände er Klingsors zweiten Zaubergarten.

Buchtipps: »Lady Chatterley« von D. H. Lawrence und »Das Dekameron« von Giovanni Boccaccio.

Le jardin enchanté de Ravello

Presque tous les génies connaissent des phases de blocage créatif. Quand Richard Wagner est arrivé à Ravello en 1880, il était embourbé dans le deuxième acte de « Parsifal » – et puis il s'est promené dans le parc d'une villa de Ravello qui lui a inspiré pour le jardin enchanté de Klingsor. Depuis, Ravello rivalise avec Bayreuth en tant que ville de Wagner. On a même fait renaître en 1953 un festival annuel de musique classique en son honneur. Parmi les initiateurs de ce festival de renom figurait Paolo Caruso, le propriétaire de l'hôtel de luxe du même nom, qui est la meilleure adresse de Ravello. Et même si l'hôtel n'appartient plus à cette famille de nos jours, il a conservé son statut. Les mélomanes désireux de côtoyer les stars wagnériennes trouveront ici un hôtel conforme à leur rang. Dans un palais du XIe siècle, le Caruso trône à 300 m au-dessus de la mer comme une loge ayant une vue fabuleuse sur la côte Amalfi. Si vous hésitez à investir dans une suite Deluxe, réservez une table sur la terrasse du restaurant du Caruso ou glissez dans l'eau de la piscine à débordement pour avoir la chance de profiter de cette vue imprenable. L'intérieur de l'hôtel est doté de plafonds voûtés et de sols en marbre, de colonnes romaines et de fresques du XVIIIe siècle : la grandezza et l'allegrezza italiennes forment ici un couple parfait. Mais le plus bel endroit au Caruso est peut-être son jardin composé de palmiers et d'orangers, de marguerites et d'hortensias ainsi que de roses ornant la tonnelle du « Belvedere ». Si Richard Wagner pouvait revenir aujourd'hui à Ravello : il trouverait ici le deuxième jardin enchanté de Klingsor.

Livres à emporter : « L'amant de Lady Chatterley » de D. H. Lawrence et « Le Décaméron » de Jean Boccace.

ANREISE	Der Flughafen Neapel ist 65 km entfernt.	ACCÈS	L'aéroport de Naples est à 65 km.
PREISE	€€€€	PRIX	€€€€
ZIMMER	24 Zimmer und 24 Suiten.	CHAMBRES	24 chambres et 24 suites.
KÜCHE	Neben dem italienischen Restaurant »Caruso« gibt es das Poolrestaurant »Belvedere« sowie zwei Bars.	RESTAURATION	Outre le restaurant « Caruso », il y a le restaurant de la piscine « Belvedere » ainsi que deux bars.
GESCHICHTE	1893 vermietete die Familie Caruso die ersten fünf Zimmer der »Pensione Belvedere«, ab 1903 hieß das Haus »Hotel Caruso«. 1999 übernahm Orient-Express das Hotel, renovierte es und feierte 2005 Neueröffnung.	HISTOIRE	La famille Caruso a loué les cinq premières chambres de la « Pensione Belvedere » en 1893 ; à partir de 1903 la maison s'est appelée « Hotel Caruso ». En 1999, Orient-Express a repris l'hôtel, l'a rénové et l'a inauguré en 2005.
X-FAKTOR	Das Gästebuch mit Widmungen von Stars wie Alexander Fleming, Humphrey Bogart und Jackie Kennedy.	LES « PLUS »	Le livre d'or avec les dédicaces d'Alexander Fleming, d'Humphrey Bogart et de Jackie Kennedy.

An Island Dream Island
Hotel Raya, Panarea, Aeolian Islands

Hotel Raya, Panarea, Aeolian Islands

An Island on an Island

Drift away to the islands of the world. Sit beneath palm trees or on rocky plateaus, your feet buried in white or black sand, and watch cinematic sunsets or mighty waves. And in the end just stay on the most beautiful isle. For most people this dream must be filed away in the "unattainable" category – for Myriam Beltrami and the artist Paolo Tilche, however, it came true. Their travels around the globe eventually led them to Panarea, the smallest of the Aeolian Islands, which in antiquity is said to have been the home of the wind god Aeolus. A simple fisherman's house was their first address – so many friends came to stay that they made a hobby into a profession and founded the Hotel Raya. Built on a slope like an Aeolian village, it looks out directly onto the nearby volcano on Stromboli – the evenings spent on the restaurant's terrace on which diners watch fiery red streams of lava flowing through the darkness are breathtaking. During the day it is not necessary to do much more here than enjoy the view and show a little leniency for the relaxed and informal service – but Mediterranean "dolce far niente" doesn't sit well with stiff five-star standards anyway. The exotic Indonesian accents, on the other hand, give a surprisingly coherent impression: Myriam Beltrami has fitted out many rooms with furniture and accessories from Bali, the island that she also discovered for herself on her journeys – as the second most beautiful isle.

Book to pack: "Journey to the Centre of the Earth" by Jules Verne.

Hotel Raya	
Via S. Pietro	
98050 Panarea	
Italy	
Tel. +39 090 983 013	
Fax +39 090 983 103	
info@hotelraya.it	
www.hotelraya.it	
Open from mid-April to the end of October	

DIRECTIONS	Panarea can be reached by hydrofoil from Naples in 4 1/2 hours.
RATES	€€
ROOMS	30 rooms in Raya Alto, 6 rooms in Raya Basso.
FOOD	Produce from organic agriculture is used for the Mediterranean meals served here.
HISTORY	Myriam Beltrami and Paolo Tilche came to Panarea in 1958 and built the Hotel Raya in the 1960s.
X-FACTOR	The boutique, in which Myriam Beltrami sells clothing, handicrafts and antiques from Bali.

Eine Insel auf der Insel

Sich zu den Inseln der Welt treiben lassen. Unter Palmen oder auf Felsplateaus sitzen, die Füße in weißem oder schwarzem Sand vergraben, kinotaugliche Sonnenuntergänge oder respekteinflößende Wellen beobachten. Und schließlich einfach auf dem schönsten Eiland bleiben. Für die meisten Menschen fällt dieser Traum in die Kategorie »unerfüllbar« – für Myriam Beltrami und den Künstler Paolo Tilche ist er jedoch wahr geworden. Ihre Reisen rund um den Globus führten sie schließlich nach Panarea, die kleinste der Äolischen Inseln, die in der Antike die Heimat des Windgottes Äolus gewesen sein sollen. Ein einfaches Fischerhaus wurde ihre erste Adresse – es kamen so viele Freunde, dass die beiden ihr Hobby zum Beruf machten und das Hotel Raya gründeten. Wie ein äolisches Dorf an den Hang gebaut, blickt es direkt auf den Vulkan von Stromboli – die Abende auf der Restaurantterrasse, an denen man feuerrote Lavaströme durch die Dunkelheit fließen sieht, sind atemberaubend. Tagsüber muss man hier nicht viel mehr tun, als die Aussicht zu genießen und etwas Nachsicht mit dem lässig-familiären Service zu haben – aber mit steifen 5-Sterne-Standards verträgt sich mediterranes »dolce far niente« eben nicht gut. Überraschend stimmig wirken dagegen die indonesisch-exotischen Akzente: Myriam Beltrami hat viele Zimmer mit Möbeln und Accessoires aus Bali ausgestattet – der Insel, die sie damals auf Reisen ebenfalls für sich entdeckt hat; als zweitschönstes Eiland.
Buchtipp: »Die Reise zum Mittelpunkt der Erde« von Jules Verne.

Une oasis de paix sur une île

Se laisser porter par les vagues vers les îles. S'asseoir sous les palmiers ou sur les rochers, les pieds enfoncés dans le sable blanc ou noir, observer des couchers de soleil dignes de cartes postales ou les vagues qui déferlent. Et puis, finalement, s'installer sur la plus belle île. Pour la plupart des gens, ce rêve reste inassouvi mais pour Myriam Beltrami et l'artiste Paolo Tilche il est devenu réalité. Leur voyage autour du monde les a finalement menés à Panarea, la plus petite des îles Eoliennes qui, dans l'Antiquité, étaient considérées comme la demeure du dieu des vents Eole. Ils ont tout d'abord vécu dans une simple maison de pêcheur et, voyant leurs amis venir en si grand nombre, ils ont décidé un jour de faire de leur hobby un métier et de créer l'Hôtel Raya. Accroché au versant de la colline comme un hameau éolien, cet hôtel donne directement sur le Stromboli. Les soirées sur la terrasse du restaurant à observer les coulées de lave rougeoyantes dans l'obscurité sont à couper le souffle. En journée, il ne faut pas s'attendre à faire beaucoup plus qu'admirer la vue et avoir un peu d'indulgence avec le service familial et nonchalant. Il est toutefois difficile de concilier le « dolce far niente » méditerranéen avec un standard cinq étoiles. Étonnamment harmonieux en revanche, les accents indonésiens et exotiques : Myriam Beltrami a aménagé de nombreuses chambres avec des meubles et accessoires de Bali, qu'elle a également découverte lors de ses voyages et qu'elle considère comme sa deuxième île de prédilection.
Livre à emporter : « Voyage au centre de la Terre » de Jules Verne.

ANREISE	Von Neapel aus erreicht man Panarea mit dem Tragflügelboot in 4,5 Stunden.	ACCÈS	De Naples, on accède à Panarea avec l'hydroglisseur en 4h 30.
PREISE	€€	PRIX	€€
ZIMMER	30 Zimmer in Raya Alto, 6 Zimmer in Raya Basso.	CHAMBRES	30 chambres à Raya Alto, 6 chambres à Raya Basso.
KÜCHE	Für die mediterranen Menüs werden Produkte aus biologisch-ökologischem Anbau verwendet.	RESTAURATION	Des produits bio sont utilisés dans les menus méditerranéens.
GESCHICHTE	Myriam Beltrami und Paolo Tilche kamen 1958 nach Panarea und bauten das Hotel Raya in den 1960ern.	HISTOIRE	Myriam Beltrami et Paolo Tilche sont arrivés à Panarea en 1958 et ont construit l'hôtel Raya dans les années 1960.
X-FAKTOR	Die Boutique, in der Myriam Beltrami Kleidung, Kunsthandwerk und Antiquitäten aus Bali verkauft.	LES « PLUS »	La boutique dans laquelle Myriam Beltrami vend des vêtements, de l'artisanat et des antiquités de Bali.

Strong Feelings on Strombo

La Locanda del Barbablù, Stromboli, Aeolian Islands

La Locanda del Barbablù, Stromboli, Aeolian Islands

Strong Feelings on Stromboli

It was one of the most famous Hollywood love stories, and it began in 1949 on Stromboli. At that time Ingrid Bergman travelled to the volcanic island to shoot the melodrama "Stromboli" with Roberto Rossellini. The actress and the director became close behind the scenes, and their affair was a scandal in conservative America, as Bergman had a husband – after filming she left him to marry Rossellini. In Italy people saw things more calmly and exhibited more business sense, too: the house in which the couple lived is still standing today and serves as first-class advertising for Stromboli. Just opposite lies La Locanda del Barbablù, which tells another "storia d'amore": the story of a friendship between the cook Neva Davanzo and the all-round talent Andrea Fabbricino. They got to know each other many years ago in Naples, moved to Venice and then to Stromboli, where they opened a bar and converted it into a hotel. It has only six rooms, charmingly and a little eccentrically furnished with colourful tiled floors and antiques – icons and paintings with maritime motifs or depictions of volcanoes tell the story of the land and the island. As the owners are the very epitome of Italian hosts, much is enjoyed together with them in Barbablù, such as the view of the volcano from the terrace, Andrea's drinks and Neva's menus, which combine the Neapolitan and the Sicilian – a culinary match that is the third love story of the trip.

Book to pack: "The Innocents Abroad" by Mark Twain.

La Locanda del Barbablù
Via Vittorio Emanuele 17
98050 Stromboli
Italy
Tel. +39 090 986 118
Fax +39 090 986 323
info@barbablu.it
www.barbablu.it
Open from the beginning of
April to the end of October

DIRECTIONS	Stromboli lies north of Sicily. It can be reached only by ship, from Naples by night ferry or speedboat (4 hours) or from Milazzo (speedboat, 2–3 hours). The Locanda is in Piscità in the north of the island, just over a mile away from the harbour.
RATES	€
ROOMS	6 rooms.
FOOD	Neva Davanzo's dishes are considered to be the best on the island.
HISTORY	In the early 20th century the hotel served as lodgings for sailors. The Locanda was opened in 1985.
X-FACTOR	The wonderful enchanted garden.

Große Gefühle

Es war eine der berühmtesten Liebesgeschichten Hollywoods, die 1949 auf Stromboli begann. Damals reiste Ingrid Bergman auf die Vulkaninsel, um mit Roberto Rossellini das Melodram »Stromboli« zu drehen. Schauspielerin und Regisseur kamen sich auch hinter den Kulissen nahe – ihre Affäre war im konservativen Amerika ein Skandal, hatte die Bergman doch einen Ehemann, den sie nach dem Dreh verließ, um Rossellini zu heiraten. In Italien sah man die Dinge gelassener und geschäftstüchtiger: Das Haus, in dem das Paar lebte, steht noch heute und macht erstklassige Werbung für Stromboli. Gleich gegenüber liegt die Locanda del Barbablù, die eine weitere »storia d'amore« erzählt: Die Geschichte der Freundschaft zwischen der Köchin Neva Davanzo und dem Allroundtalent Andrea Fabbricino. Beide lernten sich vor langen Jahren in Neapel kennen, zogen nach Venedig und dann nach Stromboli, wo sie ein Lokal eröffneten und zum Hotel ausbauten. Es umfasst nur sechs Zimmer, die mit bunten Fliesenböden und Antiquitäten charmant und ein bisschen exzentrisch eingerichtet sind – Ikonen und Gemälde mit maritimen Motiven oder Vulkandarstellungen erzählen die Historie von Land und Insel. Da die Besitzer der Inbegriff italienischer Gastgeber sind, macht man im Barbablù vieles gemeinsam, genießt den Blick auf Vulkan und Meer von der Terrasse aus, Andreas Drinks sowie Nevas Menüs, die neapolitanische und sizilianische Küche vereinen – dieses kulinarische Band ist die dritte Liebesgeschichte dieser Reise.

Buchtipp: »Die Arglosen im Ausland« von Mark Twain.

Les grands sentiments

Une des plus célèbres histoires d'amour d'Hollywood a vu le jour en 1949 sur l'île de Stromboli. Ingrid Bergman y est venue pour tourner le mélodrame « Stromboli » avec Roberto Rossellini. L'actrice et le réalisateur tombent amoureux l'un de l'autre et leur liaison fait scandale dans l'Amérique bien-pensante car l'actrice est mariée. A la fin du tournage, elle quittera son mari pour épouser Rossellini. En Italie, leur relation ne défraie pas la chronique. C'est le sens des affaires qui l'emporte : la maison dans laquelle le couple vivait, existe toujours et est une très bonne publicité pour Stromboli. Juste en face se trouve la Locanda del Barbablù, qui relate une autre storia d'amore : l'histoire d'une amitié entre la cuisinière Neva Davanzo et le talentueux Andrea Fabbricino. Ils ont fait connaissance il y a plusieurs années de cela à Naples, puis ont emménagé à Venise avant de venir s'installer à Stromboli où ils ont ouvert un bar qu'ils ont transformé en hôtel. Il ne comprend que six chambres aux carrelages multicolores, meublées à l'ancienne avec beaucoup de goût et une touche d'excentricité. Des icônes et des tableaux aux motifs marins ou représentant le volcan relatent l'histoire du pays et de l'île. Au Barbablù, les propriétaires sont fidèles à la tradition de l'hospitalité italienne : l'accueil est chaleureux et familial ; ensemble, on apprécie la vue sur le volcan et la mer depuis la terrasse, on déguste les drinks d'Andrea et les menus de Neva qui marient la cuisine napolitaine et sicilienne. Il n'y a pas de doute, cette alliance est la troisième histoire d'amour de ce voyage.

Livre à emporter : « Le voyage des innocents » de Mark Twain.

ANREISE	Stromboli liegt nördlich von Sizilien. Man erreicht es nur mit dem Schiff ab Neapel per Nachtfähre oder Schnellboot (4 Std.) oder ab Milazzo (Schnellboot, 2–3 Std.). Die Locanda steht in Piscità im Norden der Insel, 2 km vom Hafen entfernt.
PREISE	€
ZIMMER	6 Zimmer.
KÜCHE	Neva Davanzos Gerichte gelten als die besten der Insel.
GESCHICHTE	Im frühen 20. Jahrhundert diente das Haus als Herberge für Seefahrer. Die Locanda wurde 1985 eröffnet.
X-FAKTOR	Der wunderschöne verwunschene Garten.

ACCÈS	Stromboli est situé au nord de la Sicile. On y accède en bateau depuis Naples par ferry de nuit ou en vedette (4 h) ou depuis Milazzo (en vedette, en 2 à 3 h). La Locanda se trouve à Piscità au nord de l'île, à 2 km du port.
PRIX	€
CHAMBRES	6 chambres.
RESTAURATION	Les plats préparés par Neva Davanzo sont réputés pour être les meilleurs de l'île.
HISTOIRE	Au début du XXe siècle, la maison était une auberge pour les marins. La Locanda a ouvert ses portes en 1985.
LES « PLUS »	Un merveilleux jardin de conte de fées.

Luxury Living on the Land
Borgo San Marco, Fasano, Puglia

Borgo San Marco, Fasano, Puglia

Luxury Living on the Land

His ancestors went down in the annals of Apulian history as olive barons – Alessandro Amati wants to make history as an hotelier. In 1981 he purchased a fortress near Fasano with a small chapel and a mighty watchtower that was built by the Knights of Malta and once served as protection against the Turks. Amati transformed these ruins into the Borgo San Marco: a "Residenza Agrituristica" that elevates the idea of the plain and simple holiday on a farm to the level of a luxurious country estate. Vaulted ceilings, round arches and frescoes, as well as walls either whitewashed or of natural stone, call to mind both the history of the place and the rustic style of Apulia – but strong colours, linen and silk fabrics, and Middle Eastern accessories give many rooms a bohemian touch and a whiff of ethno-chic. Guests are no longer called upon to help with strenuous farm work: the former stables are now a bar, the fragrant lemon garden "l'aranceto" serves purely for relaxation, and the old watchtower functions these days as a terrace with a view across more than 250 acres of olive groves. Despite all his success as a hotel proprietor, Alessandro Amati has kept the olive press and produces the finest extra virgin oil. Naturally, the oil is used in the Borgo San Marco kitchen – and those who have developed a taste for it during their stay can buy some and take a culinary souvenir home with them.

Book to pack: "A Walk in the Dark" by Gianrico Carofiglio.

Borgo San Marco
C. da S. Angelo, 33
72015 Fasano
Italy
Tel. +39 080 439 5757
Fax +39 080 439 5757
info@borgosanmarco.it
www.borgosanmarco.it
**Open from mid-April
to mid-November**

DIRECTIONS	3 miles east of Fasano. The Brindisi and Bari airports are 25 and 37 miles away respectively.
RATES	€
ROOMS	3 double rooms, 13 suites.
FOOD	Apulian specialities are served in the restaurant.
HISTORY	The fortress dates from the 15th century; the hotel has been in existence since 2002.
X-FACTOR	In 2008 the "Borgo Aquae" spa was opened – with a Turkish hammam and hydro massage.

Der Luxus des Landlebens

Seine Vorfahren gingen als Olivenbarone in die Annalen Apuliens ein – Alessandro Amati möchte als Hotelier Geschichte schreiben. Er übernahm 1981 eine Festung bei Fasano mit kleiner Kapelle und mächtigem Wachturm, die Malteserritter einst zum Schutz gegen die Türken errichtet hatten. Die Ruine verwandelte Amati zum Borgo San Marco; einer »Residenza Agrituristica«, welche die Idee des schlichten Urlaubs auf dem Bauernhof auf luxuriöses Landgutlevel hebt. Gewölbedecken, Rundbögen und Fresken, weiß getünchte Wände, Mauern aus Naturstein erinnern an die Historie des Hauses sowie den rustikalen Stil Apuliens – kräftige Farben, Leinen- und Seidenstoffe und orientalische Accessoires verleihen vielen Räumen aber auch einen Hauch Bohème und Ethno-Chic. Bei kräftezehrenden Hofarbeiten muss kein Gast mehr mithelfen: Aus den ehemaligen Stallungen wurde eine Bar, der duftende Zitronengarten »L'Aranceto« dient ausschließlich der Entspannung, und der ehemalige Wachturm fungiert heute als Aussichtsterrasse mit Blick über 100 Hektar Olivenhaine. Denn allem Erfolg als Gastwirt zum Trotz hat Alessandro Amati die Olivenpresse behalten und produziert feinstes Öl »extra vergine«. Es wird natürlich in der Küche des Borgo San Marco verwendet – wer dort auf den Geschmack gekommen ist, kann das Öl auch kaufen und als kulinarisches Souvenir mit nach Hause nehmen.

Buchtipp: »In freiem Fall« von Gianrico Carofiglio.

Le luxe de la vie à la campagne

Les ancêtres d'Alessandro Amati sont entrés dans les annales de l'histoire des Pouilles en tant que grands producteurs d'olives. Alessandro, lui, a voulu faire ses preuves dans l'hôtellerie. En 1981, il a repris une ferme fortifiée près de Fasano, dotée d'une petite chapelle et d'une imposante tour de guet que des chevaliers de Malte avaient fait construire jadis pour se protéger des envahisseurs turcs. Amati a transformé la forteresse en ruine en Borgo San Marco, une « Residenza Agrituristica », dont l'idée est d'élever les simples vacances à la ferme au niveau du séjour luxueux dans un manoir. Les plafonds voûtés, les arcades et fresques, le badigeon blanc des murs, les pierres de taille naturelles rappellent l'histoire de la demeure ainsi que le style rustique des Pouilles mais les couleurs vives, les lins et les soies ainsi que les accessoires orientaux confèrent à de nombreuses pièces une touche bohème et de chic ethno. Les travaux harassants sont bannis depuis longtemps des lieux : un bar a été aménagé dans les anciennes écuries, le jardin embaumé des citronniers, « L'Aranceto », est réservé exclusivement au repos et l'ancienne tour de guet sert de nos jours de terrasse panoramique avec vue sur une oliveraie de plus de 100 hectares. Car, malgré sa réussite en tant qu'hôtelier, Alessandro Amati a conservé le pressoir à huile et produit une huile « extra vergine » des plus raffinées. Utilisée évidemment dans la cuisine du restaurant, elle est également en vente au domaine et fait un excellent souvenir de voyage.

Livre à emporter : « Les yeux fermés » de Gianrico Carofiglio.

ANREISE	5 km östlich von Fasano gelegen. Die Flughäfen von Brindisi und Bari sind 40 bzw. 60 km entfernt.
PREISE	€
ZIMMER	3 Doppelzimmer, 13 Suiten.
KÜCHE	Im Restaurant werden apulische Spezialitäten serviert.
GESCHICHTE	Die Festung stammt aus dem 15. Jahrhundert, das Hotel besteht seit 2002.
X-FAKTOR	2008 wurde das Spa »Borgo Aquae« eröffnet – mit türkischem Hamam und Hydromassagen.

ACCÈS	À 5 km à l'est de Fasano. Les aéroports de Brindisi et Bari sont à 40 et 60 km.
PRIX	€
CHAMBRES	3 chambres doubles, 13 suites.
RESTAURATION	Le restaurant sert des spécialités régionales.
HISTOIRE	La forteresse date du XVe siècle, l'hôtel a ouvert ses portes en 2002.
LES « PLUS »	Le spa « Borgo Aquae » a été inauguré en 2008 – avec hammam turc et hydromassages.

On the Artists' Coast

Hotel Rocamar, Cadaqués, Costa Brava

Hotel Rocamar, Cadaqués, Costa Brava

On the Artists' Coast

An "epic spot where the vertiginous cliffs of the Pyrenees drop into the sea in a grandiose geological delirium" is how Salvador Dalí described the landscape of his home, the austere Cap de Creus. The sharp-edged cliffs and gnarled trees served repeatedly as motifs for his pictures – including his most famous work "The Persistence of Memory", painted in 1931, in which melting pocket watches are depicted, one hanging from a branch, with the cliffs of the cape in the background. Dalí's life began and ended in nearby Figueres, and in the course of his career he came to Cadaqués again and again. With his wife Gala he furnished his labyrinthine home, which today is a museum. It was Dalí, too, who made the fishing village into a meeting place for artists: in his wake Picasso, Miró, Breton and Buñuel travelled to Cadaqués – which still ensures a good turnover in the galleries and souvenir shops today. Few people are aware, on the other hand, that Dalí made history not only as a Surrealist but also as an environmentalist: when the era of mass tourism began, he strongly argued against the construction of large hotel complexes – and with success: those who travel to Cadaqués today stay in individual houses such as the Rocamar, which lies somewhat outside the centre above the coast. The interior, in rustic finca style, may be more solid than spectacular – but for all that guests here enjoy unpretentious Spanish hospitality and the best view that Cadaqués has to offer: an unobstructed panorama across the Cap de Creus, Dalí's "geological delirium".

Book to pack: "The Secret Life of Salvador Dalí" by Salvador Dalí.

Hotel Rocamar
c/ Dr. Bartomeus, s/n
17488 Cadaqués, Costa Brava
Spain
Tel. +34 972 258 150 and +34 972 258 154
and +34 972 258 304
Fax +34 972 258 650
reserva@rocamar.com
www.rocamar.com
Open all year round

DIRECTIONS	Located in the easternmost region of the Iberian Peninsula, 19 miles from Figueres. The distances to the airports of Girona and Barcelona are 50 and 108 miles respectively.
RATES	€
ROOMS	72 rooms, 1 suite. Reserve a sea view, these rooms also have a balcony or a terrace.
FOOD	The restaurant serves Spanish cuisine – in summer on the veranda, which looks out over the coast.
HISTORY	The hotel was opened in 1956.
X-FACTOR	The quiet Sa Conca pebble beach directly below the hotel.

An der Küste der Künstler

Ein »geologisches Delirium, wo die Berge in einem grandiosen Taumel ins Meer stürzen«, nannte Salvador Dalí die Landschaft seiner Heimat, des herben Cap de Creus. Die scharfkantigen Klippen und knorrigen Bäume waren immer wieder Motive seiner Bilder – auch seines berühmtesten Werks »Die Beständigkeit der Erinnerung«, das er 1931 malte und auf dem vier Taschenuhren auf einem Ast und den Felsen des Kaps zerfließen. Dalís Leben begann und endete im nahen Figueres, und er kam im Lauf seiner Karriere immer wieder nach Cadaqués – mit seiner Frau Gala richtete er dort sein labyrinthartiges Wohnhaus ein, das heute ein Museum ist. Er war es auch, der aus dem Fischerort einen Künstlertreff machte: In seinem Gefolge reisten Picasso, Miró, Breton sowie Buñuel nach Cadaqués – sie sorgen in den Galerien und Souvenirshops noch heute für guten Umsatz. Dass Dalí nicht nur als Surrealist, sondern auch als Umweltschützer Geschichte schrieb, wissen dagegen nur wenige: Als die Ära des Massentourismus begann, setzte er sich gegen den Bau großer Hotelkomplexe zur Wehr – und das mit Erfolg: Wer heute nach Cadaqués fährt, wohnt in individuellen Häusern wie dem Rocamar, das etwas außerhalb des Zentrums oberhalb der Küste liegt. Das Interieur im rustikalen Finca-Stil mag eher solide denn spektakulär sein – doch dafür genießt man hier unprätentiöse spanische Gastfreundschaft und den besten Blick, den Cadaqués zu bieten hat: ein unverbautes Panorama über das Cap de Creus, Dalís geologisches Delirium.

Buchtipp: »Das geheime Leben des Salvador Dalí« von Salvador Dalí.

Sur la côte des artistes

Un endroit où la chaîne des Pyrénées, en un « délire géologique grandiose, plonge dans la mer », c'est ainsi que Salvador Dalí qualifiait le paysage de l'austère Cap de Creus, auquel il est resté toute sa vie profondément attaché. Les falaises aux arêtes vives et les arbres noueux sont un motif récurrent dans ses peintures, ainsi que dans son œuvre la plus célèbre « La Persistance de la mémoire » peinte en 1931, où quatre montres coulent sur l'unique branche d'un arbre mort et sur les rochers du Cap. Dalí a vu le jour et s'est éteint non loin de là, à Figueras. Tout au long de sa carrière, il est revenu à Cadaqués où il a aménagé avec Gala, son épouse, une maison labyrinthe qui, de nos jours, est un musée. C'est également grâce à lui que ce village de pêcheurs est devenu un repaire d'artistes. Picasso, Miró, Breton ainsi que Buñuel l'ont suivi à Cadaqués et font toujours réaliser un bon chiffre d'affaire aux galeries et boutiques de souvenirs locales. Mais Dalí n'était pas uniquement un surréaliste, ce que beaucoup ignorent c'est qu'il a également œuvré à la protection de l'environnement. Lorsque l'ère du tourisme de masse a commencé, il s'est opposé avec succès à la construction de grands complexes hôteliers. Aujourd'hui, si vous vous rendez à Cadaqués, vous résiderez dans des maisons individuelles comme le Rocamar qui surplombe la côte non loin du centre. L'intérieur de style campagnard est peut-être plus rustique que spectaculaire mais l'accueil y est chaleureux, sans prétention, et l'hôtel offre la plus belle vue de Cadaqués sur le Cap de Creus, délire géologique de Dalí, vierge de toute construction.

Livre à emporter : « La vie secrète de Salvador Dalí » de Salvador Dalí.

ANREISE	In der östlichsten Region der Iberischen Halbinsel gelegen, 30 km von Figueres entfernt. Die Distanz zu den Flughäfen von Girona und Barcelona beträgt 80 bzw. 175 km.		ACCÈS	À l'extrémité orientale de la péninsule ibérique, à 30 km de Figueras. Les aéroports de Gérone et Barcelone sont à 80 et 175 km.
PREISE	€		PRIX	€
ZIMMER	72 Zimmer, 1 Suite. Man sollte Meerblick reservieren, diese Räume besitzen auch einen Balkon oder eine Terrasse.		CHAMBRES	72 chambres, 1 suite. Réserver une chambre avec vue sur la mer, ces pièces sont dotées d'un balcon ou d'une terrasse.
KÜCHE	Das Restaurant serviert spanische Küche – im Sommer auf der Veranda, die über die Küste blickt.		RESTAURATION	Cuisine locale – servie en été sur la terrasse d'où il est possible d'admirer la côte.
GESCHICHTE	Das Hotel wurde 1956 eröffnet.		HISTOIRE	L'hôtel a ouvert ses portes en 1956.
X-FAKTOR	Der ruhige Kieselstrand Sa Conca gleich unterhalb des Hotels.		LES « PLUS »	La paisible plage de galets Sa Conca en dessous de l'hôtel.

Past and Present

Le Méridien Ra Beach Hotel & Spa, El Vendrell, Costa Daurada

Le Méridien Ra Beach Hotel & Spa, El Vendrell, Costa Daurada

Past and Present

The name itself may not sound very glamorous, but it is presented with all the effervescence and elegance of its French brother: cava, the Spanish sparkling wine made according to the methods used to produce champagne. Wine growers filled the first bottles in 1872 in Penedés – the growing region south of Barcelona that even today remains the number one in cava production. Here, legendary producers such as Freixenet or Codorníu invite guests to tastings, but those who are less keen on day trips can also be served cava simply enough – on the veranda of the "La Vinya del Penedès". The Catalan restaurant belongs to the Le Méridien Ra Beach Hotel & Spa on the Costa Daurada, the Golden Coast that owes its name to the sand that glitters gold in the sunlight. Originally the main building was a monastery of the Sant Joan de Déu Order – in 2004 architects Miquel Espinet and Antonio Ubach, along with the interior designer Teresa Ferrín, transformed it into a hotel. A whiff of the sacred still drifts through the public rooms, with their high arches – and the sparing furnishings and fittings create an impression of historical homage. At the same time, though, the present is by no means absent: wood, glass and steel, accents of colour and high tech provide for a certain urban loft ambience. Guests have a choice between rooms in the historical part and the new part of the building – those in the main building, which have their own terraces, offer especially lovely sea views. Room service is of course happy to supply a glass of cava here too – with which to toast those private holiday moments.

Book to pack: "O'Clock" by Quim Monzó.

Le Méridien Ra Beach Hotel & Spa	
Avinguda Sanatori 1	
43880 El Vendrell	
Spain	
Tel. +34 977 694 200	
Fax +34 977 692 999	
reservasra@lemeridien.com	
www.lemeridienra.com	
Open all year round (apart from	
a three week break in December)	

DIRECTIONS	34 miles southwest of Barcelona Airport.
RATES	€€
ROOMS	126 rooms and 17 suites.
FOOD	In addition to the "La Vinya del Penedès" there is the Mediterranean "Blau Marí", the "Pool Grill" with fish and meat dishes, "La Cabana Beach" with snacks as well as a bar and a lounge.
HISTORY	The monastery building was built in 1929 and the hotel, opened in 2004, was renovated at the beginning of 2007.
X-FACTOR	The thalasso spa, covering almost 2 acres – the treatments with seawater and algae are fantastic.

Geschichte und Gegenwart

Sein Name klingt nicht sehr glamourös, doch er selbst präsentiert sich ebenso prickelnd und elegant wie sein französischer Bruder: der Cava, der spanische Schaumwein, der nach Champagnermethode hergestellt wird. Die ersten Flaschen füllten Winzer 1872 im Penedés ab – der Anbauregion südlich von Barcelona, die noch heute die Nummer eins der Cavaproduktion ist. Dort laden Legenden wie Freixenet oder Codorníu zu Verkostungen ein. Wem der Sinn nicht nach Ausflügen steht, der kann sich den Cava aber auch einfach auf der Veranda des »La Vinya del Penedès« servieren lassen. Das katalanische Restaurant gehört zum Le Méridien Ra Beach Hotel & Spa an der Costa Daurada – der goldenen Küste, die ihren Namen dem im Sonnenlicht gold glänzenden Sand verdankt. Ursprünglich war das Hauptgebäude ein Kloster des Ordens Sant Joan de Déu – 2004 verwandelten es die Architekten Miquel Espinet und Antonio Ubach sowie die Interiordesignerin Teresa Ferrín in ein Hotel. Durch die öffentlichen Räume mit ihren hohen Bögen weht noch immer ein sakraler Hauch, und auch die reduzierte Ausstattung wirkt wie eine Hommage an die Geschichte. Die Gegenwart ist aber zugleich präsent: Holz, Glas und Stahl, Farbakzente und Hightech sorgen für urbanes Loft-Ambiente. Man hat die Wahl zwischen Zimmern im historischen und im neuen Teil – einen besonders schönen Meerblick eröffnen die Räume im Haupthaus, die eigene Terrassen besitzen. Auch hierher bringt der Service das Glas Cava natürlich gerne – zum Anstoßen auf private Urlaubsmomente.

Buchtipp: „Hundert Geschichten" von Quim Monzó.

Passé et présent

Son nom n'est pas très glamour, pourtant il est aussi pétillant et élégant que son cousin français : le cava est un mousseux espagnol fabriqué d'après la méthode champenoise. Il a été mis en bouteilles pour la première fois durant l'hiver 1872 par des viticulteurs à Penedés, région vinicole au sud de Barcelone et principale productrice du cava. Des producteurs de renom comme Freixenet ou Codorníu vous invitent à sa dégustation, mais si vous ne désirez pas vous rendre dans les caves, vous pouvez tout simplement vous faire servir un cava à la terrasse du « La Vinya del Penedès ». Ce restaurant catalan fait partie du complexe du Méridien Ra Beach Hotel & Spa situé sur la Costa Daurada (la côte d'or), dont le nom provient de la tonalité dorée du sable au soleil. A l'origine, le bâtiment principal était un monastère de l'ordre de Sant Joan de Déu. En 2004, les architectes Miquel Espinet et Antonio Ubach ainsi que l'architecte d'intérieur Teresa Ferrín l'ont transformé en hôtel. Les espaces communs ont gardé leur caractère sacré grâce aux grandes voûtes arquées, et la sobriété de l'ameublement rend aussi hommage à l'histoire. Mais le décor est également très contemporain : le bois, le verre, l'acier, les touches de couleur et la haute technologie lui confèrent un côté loft urbain. Vous pouvez choisir une chambre dans la partie historique ou dans la partie moderne. Les chambres du bâtiment principal disposent de terrasses avec une très belle vue sur la mer. Vous pourrez évidemment vous y faire servir un verre de cava pour trinquer à des moments privilégiés.

Livre à emporter : « Vuitanta-sis contes » de Quim Monzó.

ANREISE	55 km südwestlich vom Flughafen Barcelona entfernt.
PREISE	€€
ZIMMER	126 Zimmer und 17 Suiten.
KÜCHE	Außer dem »La Vinya del Penedès« gibt es das mediterrane »Blau Marí«, den »Pool Grill« mit Fisch- und Fleischgerichten, »La Cabana Beach« mit Snacks sowie eine Bar und eine Lounge.
GESCHICHTE	Das Klostergebäude entstand 1929, das 2004 eröffnete Hotel wurde Anfang 2007 renoviert.
X-FAKTOR	Das 7.200 qm große Thalasso-Spa – die Behandlungen mit Meerwasser und Algen sind fantastisch.

ACCÈS	À 55 km au sud-ouest de l'aéroport de Barcelone.
PRIX	€€
CHAMBRES	126 chambres et 17 suites.
RESTAURATION	Outre « La Vinya del Penedès », il y a le « Blau Marí » méditerranéen, le « Pool Grill » aux spécialités de poisson et viandes, « La Cabana Beach » avec des encas ainsi qu'un bar et un espace lounge.
HISTOIRE	Monastère construit en 1929, l'hôtel inauguré en 2004 a été rénové au début de 2007.
LES « PLUS »	Thalassothérapie et spa de 7 200 mètres carrés – excellents soins avec eau de mer et algues.

A Finca with Flair
Son Penya, San Lorenzo, Mallorca

Son Penya, San Lorenzo, Mallorca

A Finca with Flair

Putting greens under palms, fairways with views of fissured mountains, clubhouses right on the Mediterranean Sea: in the past years Mallorca has become a favourite destination for golfers – more than 100,000 of them come to the island every year to tee off on around 20 courses. In large hotels golfing holidays are often associated with glitz and glamour, celebrity tournaments and parties – those preferring to improve their handicap unobserved should book into smaller establishments, away from the centres, which attract a pleasant mix of golfers, nature lovers and romantics. One of the most enchanting hotels is Son Penya, a former finca in the northeast of Mallorca with good connections to the nearby golf courses: at the courses in Capdepera, Canyamel, Vall D'Or, Pula, Alcanada, Son Antem and Son Servera guests receive a discount on green fees. The old natural stone buildings of Son Penya have been carefully restored and stand on a huge plot of land with olive and almond trees as well as pines – the pool, the public verandas and the private terraces of all rooms enjoy fantastic views. The interior of the hotel bears the elegant signature of Toni Esteva, who offers a modern interpretation of the Mallorcan country-house style; the bathrooms, which he has placed in the rooms like showcases, are especially exquisite. A soak in the bathtub comes as a relief after 18 holes. Only Son Penya's massage comes more highly recommended: whether you choose the sportily stimulating or the completely relaxing version, it works veritable wonders.

Book to pack: "Winter in Majorca" by George Sand.

Son Penya

Camino de Son Berga, Finca Son Penya

07530 San Lorenzo, Mallorca

Spain

Tel. +34 971 826 640

Fax +34 971 826 543

sonpenya@sonpenya.com

www.esturodesonpenya.com

Open from the beginning of

February to the end of November

DIRECTIONS	Situated between San Lorenzo and Son Carrió in the east of the island, 37 miles east of the airport and 6 miles west of the next beach.
RATES	€€
ROOMS	6 rooms, 6 suites.
FOOD	The "Es S'Estador" restaurant serves Mediterranean menus and wines – exclusively for hotel guests.
HISTORY	Son Penya was opened in 2006.
X-FACTOR	6 miles away lies the conservation area of the Punta de n'Amer peninsula, where non-golfers can go on splendid walks.

Eine Finca mit Flair

Putting Greens unter Palmen, Fairways mit Blick auf zer-
klüftete Berge, Klubhäuser ganz nahe am Mittelmeer:
Mallorca ist in den vergangenen Jahren zu einem Lieblings-
ziel der Golfer geworden – mehr als 100.000 von ihnen
kommen pro Jahr auf die Insel und schlagen auf rund 20
Plätzen ab. In großen Hotels sind Golfferien oft mit Glanz
und Glamour, Promiturnieren und Partys verbunden – wer
sein Handicap lieber unbeobachtet verbessern möchte, sollte
in kleineren Häusern buchen, die abseits der Zentren liegen
und eine sympathische Mischung aus Golfern, Naturlieb-
habern und Romantikern anziehen. Eine der bezauberndsten
Adressen ist Son Penya, eine ehemalige Finca im Nordosten
Mallorcas und mit guten Beziehungen zu den nahen Golf-
plätzen: Für die Courses in Capdepera, Canyamel, Vall D'Or,
Pula, Alcanada, Son Antem und Son Servera erhalten Gäste
ermäßigte Greenfees. Die alten Natursteinbauten von Son
Penya wurden sorgsam restauriert und stehen auf einem
riesigen Grundstück mit Oliven- und Mandelbäumen sowie
Pinien – der Pool, die öffentlichen Veranden und die priva-
ten Terrassen aller Zimmer eröffnen traumhafte Ausblicke.
Innen zeigt das Haus die elegante Handschrift von Toni
Esteva, der den mallorquinischen Landhausstil modern
interpretiert; besonders raffiniert sind die Bäder, die er wie
Schaukästen in die Räume gesetzt hat. Ein Bad in der Wanne
ist nach einer Runde über 18 Loch eine Wohltat – nur die
Massage von Son Penya ist noch empfehlenswerter: Je nach
Wahl sportlich anregend oder rundum entspannend wirkt
sie wahre Wunder.
Buchtipp: »Ein Winter auf Mallorca« von George Sand.

Une finca de charme

Putting greens sous les palmiers, fairways avec vue sur des
montagnes déchiquetées, clubs proches de la Méditerranée :
Majorque est devenue, ces dernières années, la destination
préférée des golfeurs. Ils sont plus de 100 000 à venir
chaque année et à taper des balles sur les 20 terrains de l'île.
Dans les grands hôtels, les vacances conjuguées au golf sont
souvent synonymes de chic et glamour, de challenge et de
fêtes. Si vous désirez améliorer votre handicap à l'abri des
regards, mieux vaut vous éloigner des centres et réserver
dans de plus petits hôtels qui attirent un mélange sympathique de golfeurs, d'amoureux de la nature et de roman-
tiques. Une des adresses les plus charmantes est Son Penya,
une ancienne finca au nord-est de Majorque dont les propriétaires entretiennent de bonnes relations avec les terrains
de golf des alentours. Pour les parcours à Capdepera,
Canyamel, Vall D'Or, Pula, Alcanada, Son Antem et Son
Servera, les clients reçoivent des réductions sur les green
fees. Les vieux bâtiments en pierre de Son Penya, se dressant
dans un vaste domaine où poussent bon nombre d'oliviers,
d'amandiers et de pins, ont été soigneusement restaurés. La
piscine, les vérandas communes et les terrasses privées des
chambres vous offrent un panorama de rêve. A l'intérieur
de l'hôtel, on reconnaît la griffe élégante de Toni Esteva qui
a revisité le style de la maison de campagne majorquine
en le modernisant ; les salles de bains sont particulièrement
raffinées, il les a mises en scène dans les pièces comme
des vitrines. Prendre un bain dans de telles baignoires après
avoir parcouru un 18 trous est un véritable plaisir. Seul le
massage de Son Penya est encore plus agréable : au choix,
stimulant ou relaxant, il produit de vrais miracles.
Livre à emporter : « Un hiver à Majorque » de George Sand.

ANREISE	Zwischen San Lorenzo und Son Carrió im Osten der Insel gelegen, 60 km östlich vom Flughafen und 10 km westlich vom nächsten Strand entfernt.
PREIS	€€
ZIMMER	6 Zimmer, 6 Suiten.
KÜCHE	Das Restaurant »Es S'Estador« serviert mediterrane Menüs und Weine – exklusiv für Hotelgäste.
GESCHICHTE	Son Penya wurde 2006 eröffnet.
X-FAKTOR	10 km entfernt liegt das Naturschutzgebiet der Halbinsel Punta de n'Amer, wo Nichtgolfer herrlich wandern können.

ACCÈS	Entre San Lorenzo et Son Carrió à l'est de l'île, à 60 km à l'est de l'aéroport et à 10 km à l'ouest de la prochaine plage.
PRIX	€€
CHAMBRES	6 chambres, 6 suites.
RESTAURATION	Le restaurant « Es S'Estador » sert une cuisine et des vins méditerranéens, exclusivement pour les clients de l'hôtel.
HISTOIRE	Son Penya a ouvert ses portes en 2006.
LES « PLUS »	Pour les randonneurs, la réserve naturelle de la péninsule Punta de n'Amer se trouve à 10 km.

Back to the Roots
Can Pujolet, Santa Inés, Ibiza

Can Pujolet, Santa Inés, Ibiza

Back to the Roots

Ibiza – most visitors know it as an El Dorado for sun worshippers, a hot spot for night-owls and a colourful refuge for artists and individualists. But to which cultures does it owe its creative spirit? How did the people here once live? And with which landscapes did it so impress authors like Albert Camus, Jacques Prévert and Walter Benjamin that they wrote poems and books about it? Those who wish to learn about Ibiza's more than 4000-year history and get to know the regions that, even today, remain largely unchanged must leave the centres and head further afield – to places such as Can Pujolet. Once a finca, the guest house stands near the idyllic village of Santa Inés, which is protected as a historical cultural asset. Around the building, which is constructed in the simple style of the island, stretch 32 acres of land on which wine, wheat, olives, figs, pomegranates and oranges are cultivated according to organic guidelines – and bound for the hotel's own kitchen, which prepares plain, substantial fare. So fortified, guests explore the region on foot, on horseback or on a bike, receiving tips beforehand from the owners so as not to miss out on such high points as the rocky beach of Punta Galera or the hidden Cala Sardina, from which the view extends to the Spanish mainland. After the day trips, Can Pujolet's pool and the open fire promise relaxation. Anyone here missing the overcrowded beaches and clubs of Ibiza?

Book to pack: "Raoul Hausmann. Architecte – Architect. Ibiza 1933–1936" by Raoul Hausmann.

Can Pujolet	**DIRECTIONS** Located in the west of Ibiza, some 16 miles north of the airport and roughly 5 miles from the next beach.
07828 Santa Inés	
Ibiza	**RATES** €€
Spain	**ROOMS** 3 rooms, 4 suites, 1 bungalow with kitchen, 1 apartment (2 bedrooms, kitchen).
Tel. +34 971 805 170	
Fax +34 971 805 038	**FOOD** In summer guests dine in the open air; there is a dining room for use in the colder months.
info@ibizarural.com	
www.canpujolet.com	**HISTORY** The original finca dates back to the year 1900.
Open all year round	**X-FACTOR** The familial atmosphere.

Der Ursprung der Dinge

Ibiza – als Dorado für Sonnenanbeter, Szenetreff für Nachtschwärmer und regenbogenbuntes Refugium für (Lebens-)Künstler ist die Insel den meisten Besuchern bekannt. Doch welchen Kulturen verdankt sie ihr kreatives Flair? Wie haben die Menschen hier einst gelebt? Und mit welchen Landschaften hat sie Schriftsteller wie Albert Camus, Jacques Prévert und Walter Benjamin so sehr begeistert, dass sie ihr Gedichte und Bücher widmeten? Wer Ibizas mehr als 4000 Jahre lange Geschichte und seine noch heute sehr ursprünglichen Regionen kennenlernen möchte, muss die Zentren verlassen und fernere Ziele ansteuern – wie Can Pujolet. Früher eine Finca, steht das Gasthaus in der Nähe des verträumten Dorfs Santa Inés, das als historisches Kulturgut geschützt ist. Um das Gebäude im schlichten Inselstil dehnen sich 130.000 Quadratmeter Land aus, auf dem Wein, Weizen und Oliven, Feigen, Granatäpfel und Apfelsinen angebaut werden – nach ökologischen Richtlinien und für die hoteleigene Küche, die herzhafte Hausmannskost zubereitet. Gestärkt erkundet man die Umgebung zu Fuß, auf dem Pferderücken oder im Fahrradsattel und lässt sich vorher von den Besitzern die besten Tipps verraten – sonst würde man Höhepunkte wie den Felsenstrand von Punta Galera verpassen oder die versteckte Cala Sardina, von der die Sicht bis zum spanischen Festland reicht. Nach den Ausflügen versprechen der Pool von Can Pujolet sowie der offene Kamin Entspannung. Vermisst noch jemand die überfüllten Strände und Diskotheken Ibizas?

Buchtipp: »Hyle. Ein Traumsein in Spanien« von Raoul Hausmann.

L'authenticité

L'île d'Ibiza est réputée pour être l'El Dorado des fanatiques du bronzage, le rendez-vous branché des noctambules et le refuge des artistes et hippies. Mais d'où lui vient son esprit créatif ? Comment vivaient les gens sur l'île autrefois ? Et avec quels paysages a-t-elle su émerveiller des écrivains comme Albert Camus, Jacques Prévert et Walter Benjamin qui lui ont dédié poèmes et livres ? Si vous désirez découvrir l'histoire de plus de quatre mille ans d'Ibiza et ses provinces authentiques, vous devez quitter les centres touristiques et vous diriger vers des sites plus éloignés, menant par exemple à Can Pujolet. Cet hôtel, une ancienne finca, se trouve à proximité du village endormi de Santa Inés, déclaré site d'intérêt historique. Le bâtiment construit dans le style rustique ibicenco est situé sur une terre de 130 000 mètres carrés, consacrée entre autres à la culture écologique de la vigne, du blé et des olives, des figues, des grenades et des oranges. Les fruits et les légumes sont destinés à la cuisine de l'hôtel où sont préparés des plats régionaux savoureux. Réconfortés, vous partirez à la découverte des environs à pied, à cheval ou à vélo en veillant à bien demander conseil auparavant aux propriétaires. Ils vous indiqueront les meilleurs endroits à explorer comme la plage de rochers plats de Punta Galera ou la crique solitaire de Cala d'en Sardina d'où l'on peut apercevoir le continent espagnol. Au retour de vos excursions, vous pourrez vous relaxer en vous baignant dans la piscine de Can Pujolet ou en vous installant devant la cheminée. Regrettez-vous encore les plages bondées et les discothèques d'Ibiza ?

Livre à emporter : « Raoul Hausmann. Architecte – Architect. Ibiza 1933–1936 » de Raoul Hausmann.

ANREISE	Im Westen Ibizas gelegen, 26 km nördlich vom Flughafen und 8 km vom nächsten Strand entfernt.	ACCÈS	À l'ouest d'Ibiza, à 26 km au nord de l'aéroport et à 8 km de la plage.
PREISE	€€	PRIX	€€
ZIMMER	3 Zimmer, 4 Suiten, 1 Bungalow mit Küche, 1 Apartment (2 Schlafzimmer, Küche).	CHAMBRES	3 chambres, 4 suites, 1 bungalow avec cuisine, 1 studio (2 chambres, cuisine).
KÜCHE	Im Sommer wird unter freiem Himmel serviert, für die kälteren Monate steht ein Esszimmer zur Verfügung.	RESTAURATION	Service en plein air en été et salle à manger mise à disposition pour les mois les plus froids.
GESCHICHTE	Die ursprüngliche Finca stammt aus dem Jahr 1900.	HISTOIRE	La finca d'origine date de 1900.
X-FAKTOR	Das familiäre Ambiente.	LES « PLUS »	Une ambiance familiale.

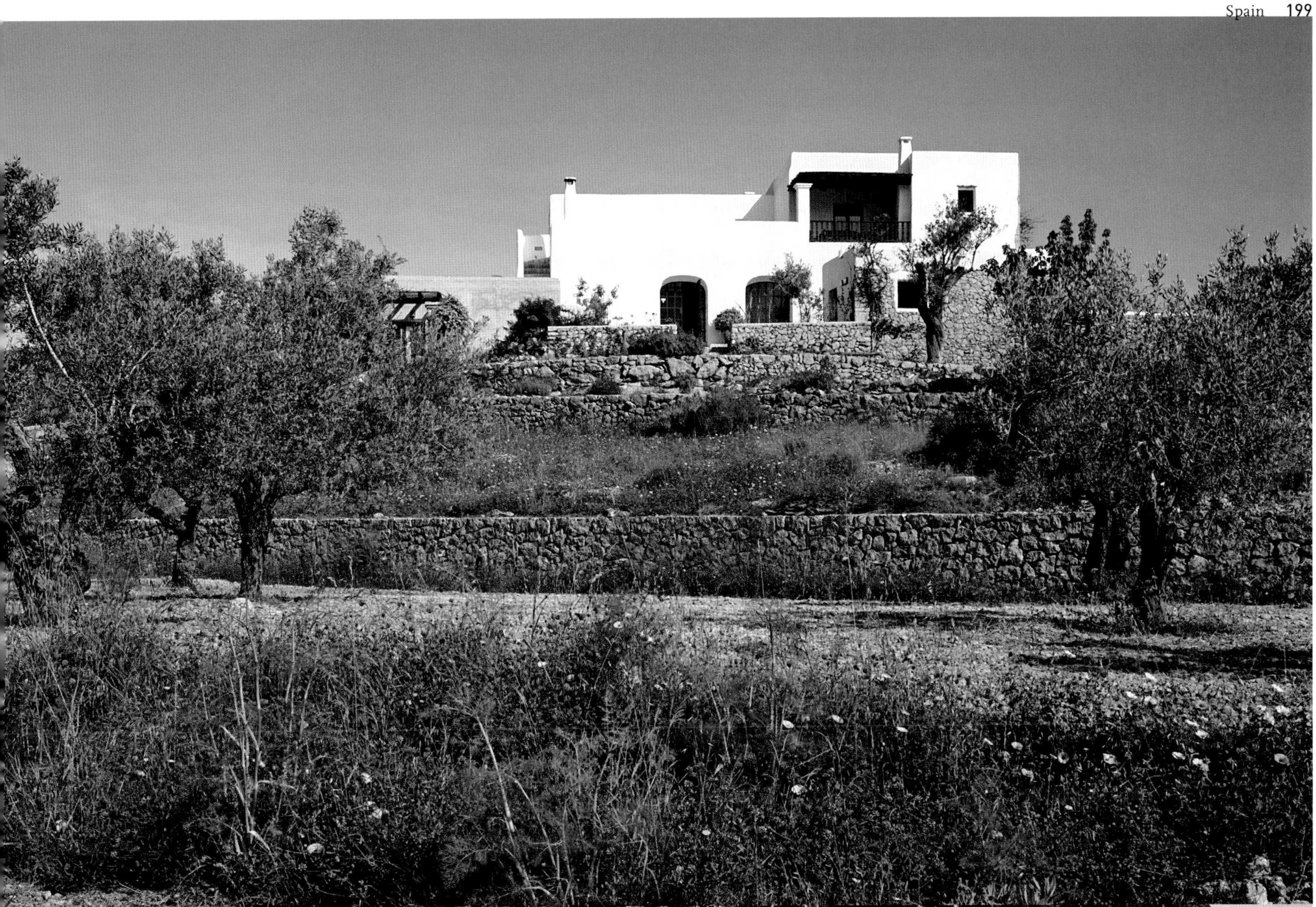

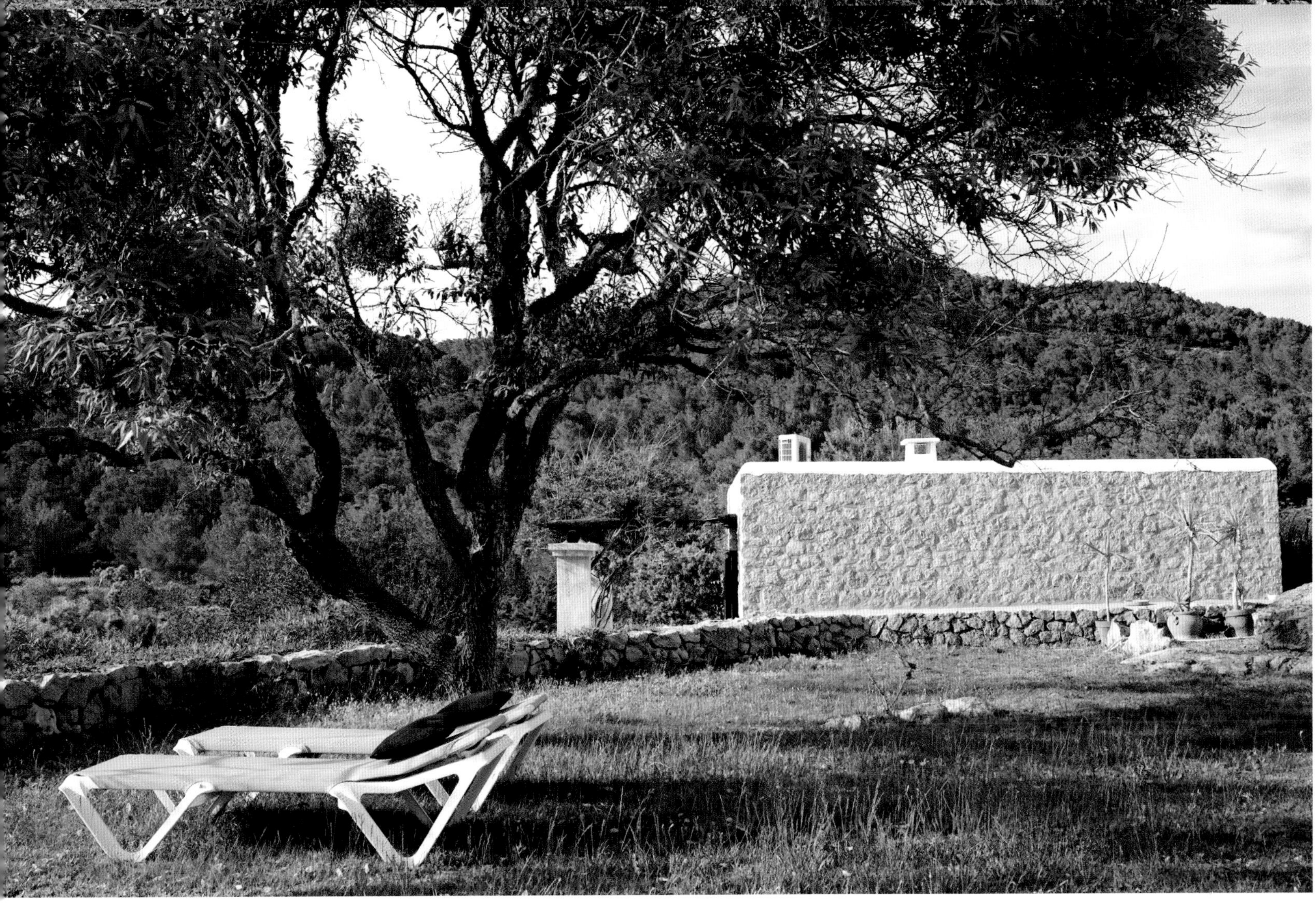

The Model House
Can Domo, Santa Eulària, Ibiza

Can Domo, Santa Eulària, Ibiza

The Model House

Its appearance is plain, simple, almost a little inconspicuous – yet it is thought out to the last detail: Ibiza's finca architecture reveals its secrets only at second glance. Then you are amazed at how many details the islanders took into account even hundreds of years ago – and how much validity these old principles still have today. The location of the hotel on the wind-protected southern slope and the three-foot-thick wall, which the heat bounces off in summer and which conserves heat in winter, make just as much sense as the flat roof on which rainwater is collected and the whitewash that keeps insects away. For those who wish to convince themselves of these and further advantages bestowed by Ibizan architecture, Can Domo is an ideal object of study. The finca, standing in the midst of ancient olive groves, dates from the 17th century and has been expertly restored by Alexandra Vermeiren and José Bernat Borras. Within the old walls, terracotta floors, ceiling beams and accessories such as a scrapped olive press tell of the past – soft fabrics, exquisite lamps and ethno-objects provide for a modern bohemian touch. In the "Cielo" suite, with its own sun deck, you live quite literally up in the heavens; those who prefer to have their feet on solid ground and like things rustic choose the "Tierra" suite, which has been set up in the former stables. Because a real finca would never stand directly by the sea – once hoards of pirates washed up on Ibiza's shores – Can Domo has no beach (the next beach is about 1 mile away), but compensation and a concession to the present day comes in the form of a marvellous pool.

Book to pack: "The Forgotten Isles" by Gaston Vuillier.

Can Domo	
Ctra. Cala Llonga, km 7,6	
Santa Eulària	
07840 Ibiza	
Spain	
Tel. +34 971 331 059	
info@candomo.com	
www.candomo.com	
Open all year round	

DIRECTIONS	Situated in a very quiet location on a hill on the east coast of Ibiza, some 13 miles from the airport.
RATES	€
ROOMS	5 rooms, 2 suites.
FOOD	Can Domo has no restaurant, but it is possible to order lunch in advance. In July and August a Thai dinner buffet is offered once a week.
HISTORY	The finca was opened as a hotel in 2000 and was redesigned by the new owners in 2005.
X-FACTOR	The beautiful Mediterranean garden.

Das Musterhaus

Sie wirkt schlicht, simpel, fast ein bisschen unscheinbar –
und ist doch bis ins Detail durchdacht: Ibizas Finca-Archi-
tektur enthüllt ihre Geheimnisse erst auf den zweiten Blick.
Dann staunt man, auf wie viele Kleinigkeiten die Insulaner
schon vor Jahrhunderten achteten – und wie viel Gültigkeit
diese alten Grundsätze noch heute haben. Die Lage eines
Hauses am windgeschützten Südhang oder die meterdicke
Mauer, die im Sommer Hitze abprallen lässt und im Winter
Wärme speichert, macht ebenso viel Sinn wie das Flachdach,
auf dem Regenwasser gesammelt wird oder die weiße
Kalktünche, die Insekten fernhält. Wer sich von diesen und
weiteren Vorteilen ibizenkischer Baukunst überzeugen
möchte, für den ist Can Domo das beste Studienobjekt. Die
inmitten uralter Olivenhaine gelegene Finca stammt aus
dem 17. Jahrhundert und wurde von Alexandra Vermeiren
und José Bernat Borras sachkundig restauriert. In den alten
Gemäuern erzählen Terrakottaböden, Deckenbalken und
Accessoires wie eine ausrangierte Olivenpresse von der
Vergangenheit – zarte Stoffe, raffinierte Lampen sowie
Ethno-Objekte sorgen für einen modernen Touch Bohème.
Wortwörtlich wie im Himmel wohnt man in der Suite
»Cielo« mit eigenem Sonnendeck; wer es lieber bodenständig und sehr rustikal mag, wählt die Suite »Tierra«, die in
den ehemaligen Stallungen eingerichtet wurde. Da eine
echte Finca niemals direkt am Meer stünde, das einst
Piraten nach Ibiza schwemmte, besitzt auch Can Domo
keinen Strand (der nächste Strand ist 2 Kilometer entfernt)
– dafür aber als Zugeständnis an die Gegenwart einen herr-
lichen Pool.

Buchtipp: »Die vergessenen Inseln« von Gaston Vuillier.

La maison modèle

Elle paraît humble, simple, presque un peu insignifiante et
pourtant elle est pensée dans les moindres détails : l'architecture de la finca d'Ibiza ne dévoile ses secrets qu'au
deuxième coup d'œil. C'est alors que l'on s'étonne des nombreux détails observés par les insulaires il y a déjà des centaines d'années et de la validité de ces anciens principes. La
situation géographique de la maison sur le versant sud à l'abri
du vent ou le murs épais d'un mètre qui, en été, renvoie la
chaleur et en hiver l'emmagasine, sont tout aussi ingénieux
que le toit plat qui recueille l'eau et les murs chaulés en
blanc qui éloignent les insectes. Si vous désirez vous laisser
convaincre des avantages de l'architecture ibicenca, Can
Domo est l'hébergement idéal. Cette finca entourée d'olive-
raies centenaires date du XVIIe siècle et a été parfaitement
restaurée par ses propriétaires, Alexandra Vermeiren et José
Bernat Borras. Entre ces vieux murs, les sols en terracota, les
solives et les accessoires tel le vieux pressoir à olives parlent
du passé. Des étoffes délicates, des lampes raffinées et des
objets ethniques donnent une touche bohème et moderne
à l'ensemble. Vous pourrez habiter dans la suite « cielo »
véritablement céleste avec sa terrasse solarium, mais si vous
êtes plus terre à terre et préférez une chambre plus rustique,
vous choisirez la suite « tierra », qui a été aménagée dans
les anciennes écuries. Comme une vraie finca est toujours
éloignée de la mer, infestée autrefois de pirates, Can Domo
ne dispose pas de plage (la plus proche est à 2 kilomètres).
Toutefois, elle possède une superbe piscine, en accord avec
les temps présents.

Livre à emporter : « Les îles oubliées » de Gaston Vuillier.

ANREISE	Sehr ruhig an einem Hügel an der Ostküste Ibizas gele-gen, 20 km vom Flughafen entfernt.
PREISE	€
ZIMMER	5 Zimmer, 2 Suiten.
KÜCHE	Can Domo besitzt kein Restaurant, man kann jedoch Lunch vorbestellen. Im Juli und August wird einmal wöchentlich ein Thai-Dinnerbuffet angeboten.
GESCHICHTE	Die Finca wurde 2000 als Hotel eröffnet und 2005 von ihren neuen Besitzern neu designt.
X-FAKTOR	Der wunderschöne mediterrane Garten.

ACCÈS	Endroit très tranquille, finca perchée sur une colline sur la côte est d'Ibiza, à 20 km de l'aéroport.
PRIX	€
CHAMBRES	5 chambres, 2 suites.
RESTAURATION	Le Can Domo ne dispose pas de restaurant mais fait table d'hôtes sur réservation. En juillet et août, un dîner thaï avec buffet est proposé une fois par semaine.
HISTOIRE	Cette finca a ouvert ses portes en tant qu'hôtel en 2000 et a été redécorée par ses nouveaux propriétaires en 2005.
LES « PLUS »	Le magnifique jardin méditerranéen.

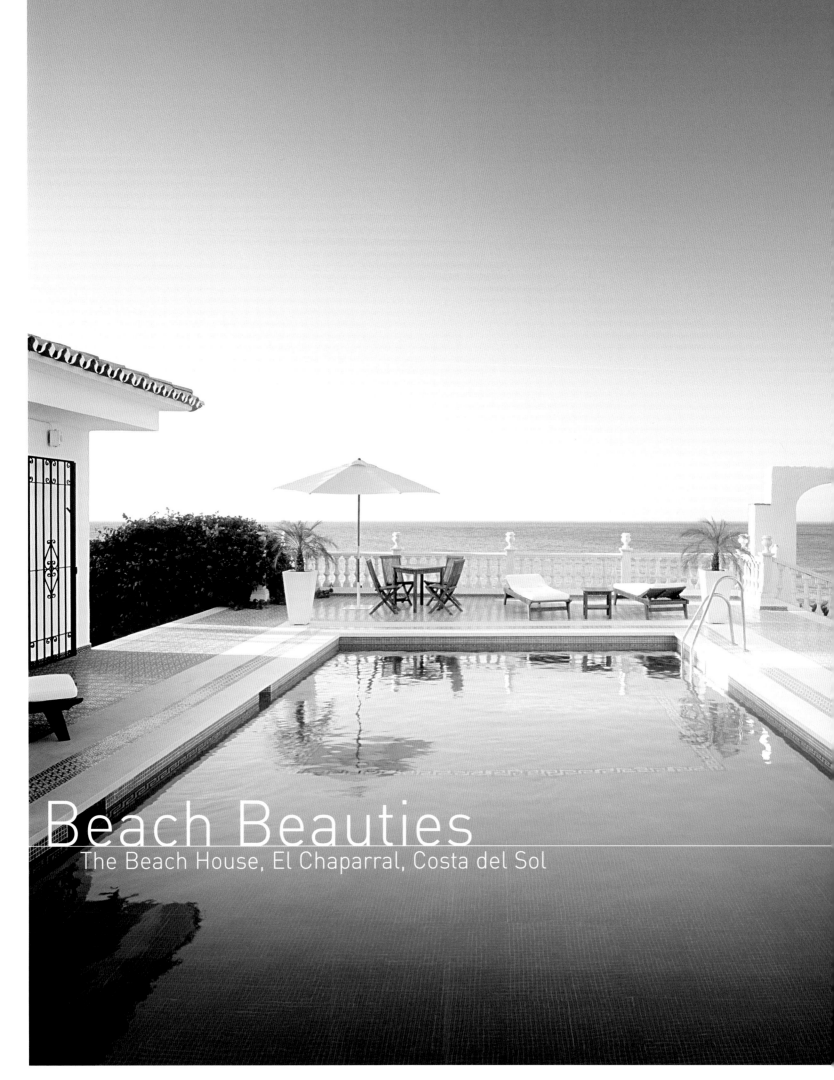

Beach Beauties
The Beach House, El Chaparral, Costa del Sol

The Beach House, El Chaparral, Costa del Sol

Beach Beauties

A design that is as stylish as it is simple, as aesthetic as it is functional, as elegant as it is affordable, that sets great store by selected materials and high quality and that stands for quality of life: in all likelihood this description makes you think of Scandinavia, not of Spain. And yet there is a very successful example of Scandinavian design on the Spanish coast – on the Costa del Sol between Málaga and Marbella. It is here that the Swede Kjell Sporrong has fitted out The Beach House, which lies exactly where the name implies and with a mere ten rooms possesses all the charm of a private villa. In the interior warm chocolate tones contrast with gleaming white – the nicest rooms look directly out onto the sea (they are at the same time the quietest; here, the nearby coastal road is inaudible). Outside, northern clarity is combined with southern accents: the pool is on the patio, which exudes the feel of Andalusia, and is bordered with wonderful blue and white tiles. In the evening the water is atmospherically illuminated and makes a romantic place for a glass of wine before dinner. The Beach House itself has no restaurant – but your hosts Carina and Stefan Andersson, who, like the designer, come from Sweden, are happy to disclose their favourite culinary addresses. And when you get back, a nightcap awaits you in The Beach House – accompanied by the sound of the sea or the songs on the hotel's own chill-out CD.

Books to pack: "The House of Bernarda Alba" by Federico García Lorca and "In Her Absence" by Antonio Muñoz Molina.

The Beach House	
Urb El Chaparral	
CN-340, km 203	
29648 Mijas Costa	
Spain	
Tel./Fax +34 95 249 4540	
info@beachhouse.nu	
www.beachhouse.nu	
Open all year round	

DIRECTIONS	Located somewhat outside the village of La Cala on a quiet section of beach some 19 miles southwest of Málaga Airport.
RATES	€€
ROOMS	10 rooms.
FOOD	Breakfast is served at the pool, with a sea view, or in the lounge.
HISTORY	The Beach House was opened in 2001.
X-FACTOR	The hotel's own boutique, in which you can purchase numerous Beach House design objects; for example crockery, works of art and the CDs "The Beach House Marbella Volumes 1 & 2".

Strandschönheiten

Ein Design, das ebenso stilvoll wie schlicht, ebenso ästhetisch wie funktional, ebenso elegant wie erschwinglich ist, das Wert auf ausgesuchte Materialien und hohe Qualität legt und ein Stück Lebensqualität symbolisiert: Bei dieser Beschreibung denkt man ziemlich sicher an Skandinavien und wahrscheinlich nicht an Spanien. Und doch steht ein sehr gelungenes Beispiel skandinavischen Designs an der spanischen Küste – an der Costa del Sol zwischen Málaga und Marbella. Hier hat der Schwede Kjell Sporrong das Beach House eingerichtet, das, wie sein Name verspricht, unmittelbar am Strand liegt und mit nur zehn Zimmern den Charme einer privaten Villa besitzt. Innen kontrastieren warme Schokoladentöne und strahlendes Weiß – die schönsten Räume blicken direkt aufs Meer (sie sind zugleich die ruhigsten, die nahe Küstenstraße ist hier überhaupt nicht zu hören). Außen verbindet sich die nordische Klarheit mit südlichen Akzenten: Der Pool liegt im andalusisch angehauchten Patio und ist mit wunderschönen blau-weißen Fliesen eingefasst. Abends wird das Schwimmbecken stimmungsvoll beleuchtet und ist ein romantischer Platz für ein Glas Wein vor dem Dinner. Das Beach House selbst besitzt kein Restaurant – doch die Gastgeber Carina und Stefan Andersson, die wie der Designer aus Schweden stammen, verraten gerne ihre kulinarischen Lieblingsadressen. Nach der Rückkehr gibt es im Beach House noch einen Schlummerdrink – begleitet vom Rauschen des Meeres oder den Songs der hoteleigenen Chill-out-CD.

Buchtipps: »Bernarda Albas Haus« von Federico García Lorca und »Siesta mit Blanca« von Antonio Muñoz Molina.

Un beau mariage

Un design, aussi simple que de bon goût, esthétique et fonctionnel, élégant et abordable, qui accorde de l'importance à des matériaux de choix et à l'excellence et qui symbolise une certaine qualité de vie : une telle description fait penser immédiatement à la Scandinavie et certainement pas à l'Espagne. Et pourtant, il s'agit ici d'un exemple très réussi de design scandinave situé sur une côte espagnole, la Costa del Sol entre Málaga et Marbella. C'est là que le Suédois Kjell Sporrong a aménagé l'hôtel Beach House qui, comme son nom l'indique, se trouve au bord de la mer. Le Beach House ne comprend que dix chambres et a su préserver ainsi le charme d'une villa privée. A l'intérieur, des tons chauds de chocolat contrastent avec un blanc éclatant. Les plus belles pièces donnent directement sur la mer (elles sont également les plus calmes car plus éloignées de la route côtière). A l'extérieur, la clarté nordique s'allie aux accents méditerranéens : la piscine se trouve dans le patio de style andalou et est bordée de magnifiques carreaux bleus et blancs. Le soir, le bassin joliment éclairé est l'endroit idéal pour boire un verre de vin dans une ambiance romantique avant le dîner. Le Beach House ne possède pas de restaurant mais les hôtes de ces lieux Carina et Stefan Andersson, tous deux suédois comme le designer, vous communiqueront volontiers de bonnes adresses. A votre retour au Beach House, vous pourrez prendre un dernier verre en écoutant le mugissement des vagues ou les chansons du CD chill-out de l'hôtel.

Livres à emporter : « La maison de Bernarda Alba » de Federico García Lorca et « En l'absence de Blanca » d'Antonio Muñoz Molina.

ANREISE	Etwas außerhalb des Dorfes La Cala an einem ruhigen Strandabschnitt gelegen, 30 km südwestlich vom Flughafen Málaga entfernt.
PREISE	€€
ZIMMER	10 Zimmer.
KÜCHE	Das Frühstück wird am Pool mit Meerblick oder in der Lounge serviert.
GESCHICHTE	The Beach House wurde 2001 eröffnet.
X-FAKTOR	Die hoteleigene Boutique, in der man viele Designobjekte des Beach House kaufen kann; zum Beispiel Geschirr, Kunstwerke und die CDs »The Beach House Marbella Volume 1 & 2«.

ACCÈS	Un peu en dehors du village de La Cala, sur une portion de plage tranquille, à 30 km au sud-ouest de l'aéroport de Málaga.
PRIX	€€
CHAMBRES	10 chambres.
RESTAURATION	Petit-déjeuner servi au bord de la piscine avec vue sur la mer ou dans le lounge.
HISTOIRE	Le Beach House a ouvert ses portes en 2001.
LES « PLUS »	La boutique de l'hôtel où l'on peut acheter de nombreux objets design du Beach House ; par exemple de la vaisselle, des œuvres d'art et les CD « The Beach House Marbella Volume 1 & 2 ».

A Following Wind
Hotel Dos Mares, Tarifa, Costa de la Luz

Hotel Dos Mares, Tarifa, Costa de la Luz

A Following Wind

The locals call them "los locos por el viento" (those who are crazy for the wind) – the surfers who ride the waves off Tarifa, leaping over white, foaming crests of spray or being hoisted up into the air by their kite canopies. Tarifa is the southernmost town of the European mainland and at the same time a capital of the wind: almost all year round the Levante and Poniente blow here – one a warm east wind from the Mediterranean Sea, the other a cooler west wind from the Atlantic – and really gather momentum through the narrow Strait of Gibraltar; only off the coasts of Hawaii and Fuerteventura do surfers find comparable havens. Among Tarifa's best spots is the sandy beach of Los Lances, where Dutchman Robert Van Looy, one of Tarifa's tourism pioneers who came to Spain in the 1960s, opened the Hotel Dos Mares. Guests stay either in the rooms of the main building or rent one of the pretty bungalows, painted sky blue, sunshine yellow or red-brown, which look directly onto the sea. The colourful design of all the rooms is inspired by nearby Morocco (North Africa is only some 9 miles away), and the ambience is wholly in accordance with the relaxed chill-out character of Tarifa. For this reason and because the hotel has its own riding stables, families with children also feel at home here – but the majority of guests are young surfers, who are perfectly happy as soon as they get out onto the water with a following wind.

Book to pack: "Leaving Tangier" by Tahar Ben Jelloun.

Hotel Dos Mares
Ctra. Cádiz-Málaga, km 79,5
11380 Tarifa
Spain
Tel. +34 956 68 40 35
Fax +34 956 68 10 78
info@dosmareshotel.com
www.dosmareshotel.com
Open all year round

DIRECTIONS	Located on the Costa de la Luz, 112 miles southwest of Málaga Airport.
RATES	€
ROOMS	8 rooms, 4 suites, 34 bungalows.
FOOD	Spanish-Moroccan dishes are served in the "Restaurante Yamani"; in addition there is the "Café Dos Vientos", a cafeteria and a snack bar.
HISTORY	The hotel was opened in 1975. The surf school belonging to the hotel has been in existence since 1993.
X-FACTOR	From the pool on a clear day it is possible to see all the way to Morocco.

Den Wind im Rücken

Die Einheimischen nennen sie »los locos por el viento« (die nach dem Wind Verrückten) – die Surfer, die vor Tarifa durch die Wellen jagen, über weiß schäumende Gischtkämme springen oder sich von ihrem Kite-Schirm in den Himmel ziehen lassen. Tarifa ist die südlichste Stadt des europäischen Festlandes und zugleich eine Hauptstadt des Windes: Nahezu rund ums Jahr wehen hier Levante und Poniente – der eine ein warmer Ostwind vom Mittelmeer, der andere ein kühlerer Westwind vom Atlantik – und kommen über der engen Straße von Gibraltar so richtig in Schwung; nur vor den Küsten von Hawaii und Fuerteventura finden Surfer vergleichbare Paradiese. Einer der besten Spots von Tarifa ist der Sandstrand Los Lances, wo Robert Van Looy, der in den 1960ern aus Holland nach Spanien kam und zu den Tourismuspionieren Tarifas gehört, das Hotel Dos Mares eröffnet hat. Hier wohnt man entweder in den Zimmern des Hauptgebäudes oder mietet einen der hübschen Bungalows, die himmelblau, sonnengelb oder rotbraun gestrichen sind und direkt aufs Meer schauen. Das farbenfrohe Design aller Räume ist vom nahen Marokko inspiriert (die Entfernung nach Nordafrika beträgt gerade einmal 14 Kilometer), und das Ambiente entspricht ganz dem gelassenen Chill-out-Charakter von Tarifa. Deshalb und wegen des hoteleigenen Reitstalls fühlen sich hier auch Familien mit Kindern wohl – die meisten Gäste sind jedoch junge Surfer, die wunschlos glücklich sind, sobald sie auf dem Meer sind und den Wind im Rücken haben.

Buchtipp: »Verlassen« von Tahar Ben Jelloun.

Le vent en poupe

Les autochtones les surnomment « los locos por el viento » (les fous du vent) : ce sont les surfeurs ou kitesurfeurs qui glissent à toute vitesse sur les vagues devant Tarifa, sautent au-dessus des crêtes d'écume blanche ou se laissent tracter vers le ciel par leur aile. Tarifa est la ville la plus méridionale du continent européen et en même temps une capitale du vent. Deux types de vents y soufflent presque toute l'année : le levante et le poniente. L'un est un vent d'est et chaud venant de la Méditerranée et l'autre un vent d'ouest plus froid venant de l'Atlantique. Générés par un goulet, ils prennent leur élan dans le détroit de Gibraltar ; les surfeurs ne trouvent de tels paradis que sur les côtes d'Hawaii et de Fuerteventura. Un des meilleurs endroits est la plage de sable fin de Los Lances où Robert Van Looy, un des premiers touristes hollandais venu dans les années 1960, a ouvert l'hôtel Dos Mares. Ici, vous pourrez séjourner dans les chambres du bâtiment pincipal ou louer un des jolis bungalows peints en bleu ciel, jaune soleil ou rouge brun et donnant directement sur la mer. Dans toutes les pièces, le design haut en couleurs est d'inspiration marocaine (l'Afrique du Nord ne se trouvant qu'à une quinzaine de kilomètres) et l'ambiance reflète l'esprit totalement décontracté et chill-out de Tarifa. L'hôtel possède également des chevaux qu'il est possible de louer : un atout pour les familles avec enfants. Toutefois, la plupart des clients sont de jeunes surfeurs qui sont comblés dès qu'ils chevauchent des vagues et ont le vent en poupe.

Livre à emporter : « Partir » de Tahar Ben Jelloun.

ANREISE	An der Costa de la Luz gelegen, 180 km südwestlich vom Flughafen Málaga entfernt.
PREISE	€
ZIMMER	8 Zimmer, 4 Suiten, 34 Bungalows.
KÜCHE	Im »Restaurante Yamani« wird spanisch-marokkanisch gekocht, zudem gibt es das »Café Dos Vientos«, eine Cafeteria und eine Snackbar.
GESCHICHTE	Das Hotel wurde 1975 eröffnet. Seit 1993 besteht die hauseigene Surfschule.
X-FAKTOR	Vom Pool aus blickt man an klaren Tagen bis nach Marokko.

ACCÈS	Sur la Costa de la Luz, à 180 km au sud-ouest de l'aéroport de Málaga.
PRIX	€
CHAMBRES	8 chambres, 4 suites, 34 bungalows.
RESTAURATION	Le « Restaurante Yamani » propose une cuisine espagnole et marocaine, mais vous trouverez aussi sur place le « Café Dos Vientos », une cafétéria et un snack-bar.
HISTOIRE	L'hôtel a ouvert ses portes en 1975. Il dispose aussi d'une école de surf depuis 1993.
LES « PLUS »	Par temps clair, de la piscine, on peut apercevoir les côtes marocaines.

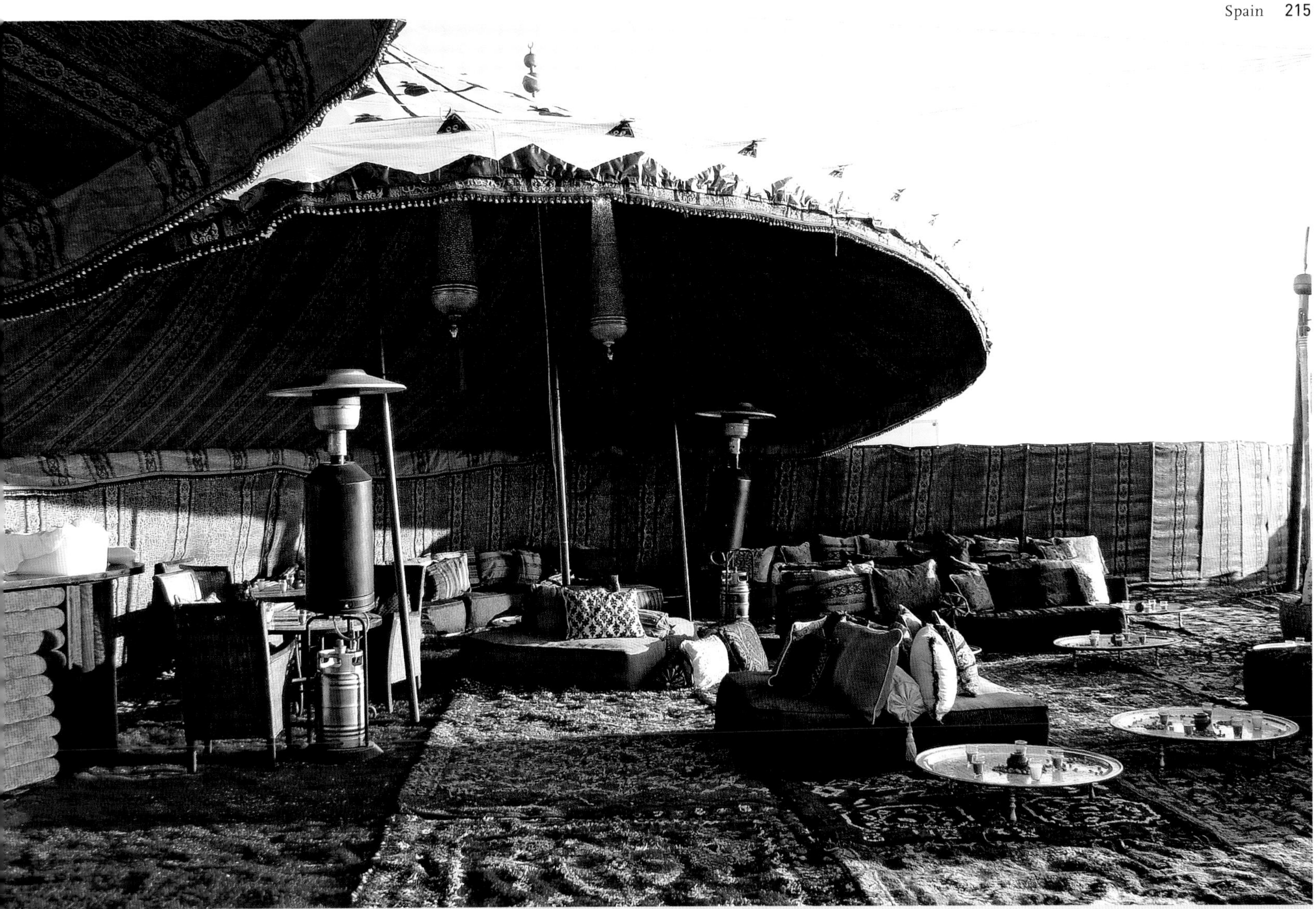

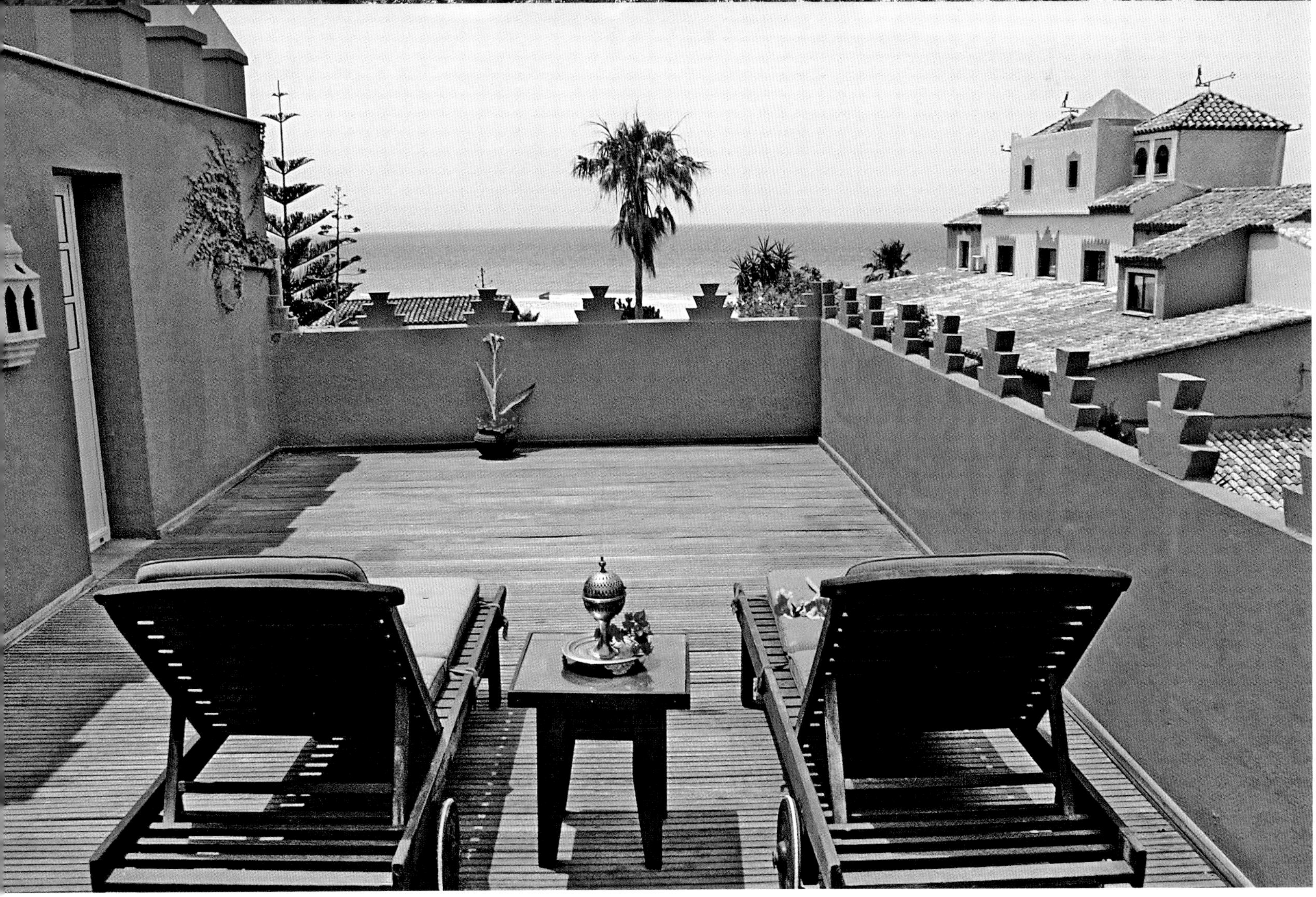

An Island Idyll

La Villa, Lopud Island

La Villa, Lopud Island

An Island Idyll

Uncharted territory on the map of Europe – discovering an unknown destination would make anyone's heart beat a little faster, especially as today just about every place has been catalogued, photographed and documented a hundred times. Lopud is among the exceptions: up until now, just a few visitors and reporters have found their way to the island off the Dalmatian coast not far from Dubrovnik. Those who do make it can enjoy the marvellous landscape in absolute peace and quiet – thanks to the mild climate and a freshwater spring subtropical plants thrive here – and take a journey back in time. Greek and Roman ruins recall the first settlers, magnificent summer residences bear witness to the region's 15th-century heyday, when Lopud was headquarters of the Ragusan Republic and home to mighty shipowners, and more than 30 churches and chapels are the legacy of two monasteries. Between a small beach and the botanical garden stands "La Villa", the prettiest accommodation on the island, a building with a grand façade and only eight rooms. The standard rooms are plain – it pays to reserve a superior room with French windows that look out onto the Adriatic (the blue room even boasts a terrace facing the sea and is especially tastefully furnished). The hosts spoil their guests with personal service: They conjure up delicious menus on request, disclose the best spots for diving and head for hidden beaches and idyllic bays in the hotel's own boat.

Book to pack: "Black Lamb and Grey Falcon: A Journey Through Yugoslavia" by Rebecca West.

La Villa
Iva Kuljevana 33
20222 Lopud
Croatia
Tel. +385 91 322 0126
contact@lavilla.com.hr
www.lavilla.com.hr
Open from the beginning of
April to the end of November

DIRECTIONS	The crossing from Dubrovnik to Lopud takes 30 to 60 min. The island is car free; guests are picked up by the owners at the harbour.
RATES	€
ROOMS	8 rooms (without telephone and television).
FOOD	"La Villa" normally serves breakfast; dinner on request only.
HISTORY	A manor house stood here as early as the 16th century. Today's villa was built in 1862, redeveloped in the 1980s and renovated in 2004.
X-FACTOR	It is possible to rent the whole villa.

Inselidyll

Auf der Landkarte Europas einen weißen Fleck, ein noch unbekanntes Reiseziel zu entdecken, lässt das Herz schneller schlagen – ist heute doch so gut wie jeder Ort hundertfach katalogisiert, fotografiert und dokumentiert. Lopud zählt zu den Ausnahmen: Den Weg auf die Insel vor Dalmatiens Küste, nicht weit von Dubrovnik entfernt, haben bislang noch nicht viele Besucher und Berichterstatter gefunden. Wer es schafft, kann in aller Ruhe eine herrliche Landschaft genießen – dank des milden Klimas sowie einer Süßwasserquelle gedeihen hier subtropische Pflanzen – und in die Geschichte zurückreisen: Griechische und römische Ruinen erinnern an die ersten Siedler, prächtige Sommerresidenzen an die Blütezeit im 15. Jahrhundert, als Lopud Hauptsitz der Republik Ragusa war und Heimat mächtiger Reeder, und mehr als 30 Kirchen und Kapellen sind Erbe zweier Klöster. Zwischen einem kleinen Strand und dem botanischen Garten steht mit »La Villa« die hübscheste Unterkunft der Insel, ein Bau mit herrschaftlicher Fassade und gerade einmal acht Zimmern. Die Standardräume sind schlicht – es lohnt sich, ein Superior-Zimmer mit französischen Fenstern zu reservieren, die auf die Adria blicken. Das Blaue Zimmer besitzt sogar eine Terrasse zum Meer und ist besonders geschmackvoll eingerichtet. Die Gastgeber verwöhnen ihre Gäste mit persönlichem Service: Sie zaubern auf Wunsch delikate Menüs, verraten die besten Tauchspots oder steuern an Bord des hauseigenen Boots versteckte Strände und idyllische Buchten an.

Buchtipps: »Schwarzes Lamm und grauer Falke: eine Reise durch Jugoslawien« von Rebecca West und »Warum ich euch belogen habe« von Julijana Matanovic.

Une île idyllique

Une tache blanche sur la carte de l'Europe, une destination inconnue qui reste à découvrir. Voilà qui excite notre curiosité, car presque tous les lieux sont aujourd'hui catalogués, photographiés et documentés des centaines de fois. Lopud fait partie des exceptions : peu de touristes et reporters ont trouvé jusqu'ici le chemin menant à cette île de la côte dalmatienne, à proximité de Dubrovnik. Les curieux qui s'y aventurent peuvent admirer le paysage en toute tranquillité – grâce à la douceur du climat et la présence d'une source, des plantes subtropicales y poussent – et aussi effectuer un voyage dans le temps : des ruines grecques et romaines évoquent les premiers occupants, de magnifiques résidences d'été rappellent l'époque florissante du XVe siècle, quand Lopud était le siège de la République de Raguse où résidaient de puissants armateurs, et plus de 30 églises et chapelles sont l'héritage de deux monastères. Entre une petite plage et le jardin botanique se dresse « La Villa », le plus bel hôtel de l'île, un bâtiment arborant une façade seigneuriale et n'abritant que huit chambres. Les pièces standard sont simples. Il vaut mieux réserver une chambre supérieure dont les grandes fenêtres donnent sur l'Adriatique (la chambre bleue possède même une terrasse avec vue sur la mer et est aménagée avec beaucoup de goût). Les hôtes s'occupent personnellement de leurs clients : ils préparent de bons repas sur commande et ils n'hésitent pas à révéler où sont les meilleurs spots de plongée quand ils ne se dirigent pas, à bord de leur bateau, vers de petites criques idylliques ou des plages cachées.

Livre à emporter: « Agneau noir et faucon gris : un voyage à travers la Yougoslavie » de Rebecca West.

ANREISE	Die Überfahrt von Dubrovnik nach Lopud dauert 30 bis 60 min. Die Insel ist autofrei, am Hafen wird man von den Besitzern abgeholt.	ACCÈS	La traversée de Dubrovnik à Lopud dure de 30 à 60 min. Pas de voitures sur l'île, les propriétaires viennent vous chercher au port.
PREISE	€	PRIX	€
ZIMMER	8 Zimmer (ohne Telefon und Fernseher).	CHAMBRES	8 chambres (sans téléphone et sans télévision).
KÜCHE	Regulär serviert »La Villa« Frühstück, Dinner nur auf Anfrage.	RESTAURATION	Petit déjeuner, dîner sur commande.
GESCHICHTE	Schon im 16. Jahrhundert stand hier ein Herrenhaus. Die heutige Villa wurde 1862 erbaut und in den 1980ern saniert sowie 2004 renoviert.	HISTOIRE	À cet emplacement, il y avait déjà un manoir au XVIe siècle. L'actuelle villa a été construite en 1862, restaurée dans les années 1980 puis rénovée en 2004.
X-FAKTOR	Die komplette Villa kann exklusiv gemietet werden.	LES « PLUS »	Possibilité de louer toute la villa.

Cinematic
Bratsera Hotel, Hydra

Bratsera Hotel, Hydra

Cinematic

In the 1960s, all hell broke loose on Hydra – or, more precisely, all Hollywood: whether Audrey Hepburn or Greta Garbo, Anthony Quinn or Henry Fonda – at the time everybody of note in the American Dream Factory holidayed on the island. The European jet set, too, dropped anchor in the Saronic Gulf – arriving on the yachts of Onassis or Sachs – and artists found inspiration here. It was on Hydra that Leonard Cohen fell in love with the woman for whom he later wrote "So Long Marianne". The reason for this surge of holidaymakers was a movie from the year 1957: "Boy on a Dolphin" featured breathtaking shots of the island and the young Sophia Loren as the sponge diver Phaedra. Sponge diving was in fact once one of the most important sources of income for the inhabitants of the island; in the mid-19th century Hydra possessed one of the largest sponge factories in the region. It is not only still possible to view the building today, but also to live in it, as it houses the enchanting Bratsera Hotel – named after the "bratsera", the ship on which the sponge divers could rest. The architect Dimitris Papacharalampous has done a fantastic job of renovating the complex, giving the lobby a touch of industrial loft atmosphere and fitting out the rooms with local wood and stone (the mezzanine rooms have come off particularly well). His style combines tradition and modernity, is simple but sophisticated, at once down-to-earth and glamorous – the Bratsera would make the loveliest backdrop for the next Hydra-based movie.

Book to pack: "Flowers for Hitler" by Leonard Cohen.

Bratsera Hotel	
Hydra 18040	
Greece	
Tel. +30 22980 539 71	
Fax +30 22980 536 26	
bratsera@yahoo.com	
www.bratserahotel.com	
Open from mid-March	
to the end of October	

DIRECTIONS	From Piraeus, Hydra is reached by ferry in 1 1/2 hrs. The island is car free; the hotel is a 2 min walk from the harbour.
RATES	€€
ROOMS	21 rooms, 5 suites.
FOOD	Greek and Mediterranean specialities are on the menu in the restaurant; diners eat on the veranda in summer.
HISTORY	The sponge factory was built by Nickolaos Verneniotis in 1860; the hotel opened in 1994.
X-FACTOR	The pool and the flower-filled garden are veritable oases.

Filmreif

In den 1960ern war auf Hydra die Hölle los – oder besser gesagt Hollywood: Ob Audrey Hepburn oder Greta Garbo, Anthony Quinn oder Henry Fonda – auf der Insel urlaubte damals jeder, der in der amerikanischen Traumfabrik Rang und Namen hatte. Auch der europäische Jetset ging im Saronischen Golf vor Anker – angereist auf den Jachten von Onassis oder Sachs – und Künstler fanden hier Inspiration: Leonard Cohen verliebte sich auf Hydra in die Frau, für die er später »So Long Marianne« schrieb. Auslöser dieser Reisewelle war ein Kinofilm des Jahres 1957 gewesen: »Der Junge auf dem Delphin« mit atemberaubenden Aufnahmen der Insel und der jungen Sophia Loren als Schwammfischerin Phaedra. Die Schwammfischerei war früher tatsächlich eine der wichtigsten Einkommensquellen der Hydrioten; Mitte des 19. Jahrhunderts besaß das kleine Eiland eine der größten Schwammfabriken der Region. Man kann das Gebäude noch heute besichtigen und sogar bewohnen, denn es beherbergt das zauberhafte Bratsera Hotel – benannt nach der »bratsera«, dem Schiff, auf dem sich die Schwammtaucher ausruhen konnten. Der Architekt Dimitris Papacharalampous hat den Komplex fantastisch renoviert, der Lobby einen Hauch Industrieloft-Atmosphäre verliehen und die Räume mit einheimischem Holz und Stein ausgestattet (die Mezzanin-Zimmer sind besonders gelungen). Sein Stil verbindet Tradition und Moderne, ist schlicht und sophisticated, bodenständig und glamourös zugleich – das Bratsera wäre die schönste Kulisse für den nächsten Kinofilm aus Hydra.

Buchtipp: »Blumen für Hitler« von Leonard Cohen.

Digne d'un film

Dans les années 1960, tout Hollywood était à Hydra. Que ce soit Audrey Hepburn ou Greta Garbo, Anthony Quinn ou Henry Fonda, tous ceux qui étaient devenus célèbres grâce à l'usine à rêve américaine passaient leurs vacances sur l'île. Même la jet-set européenne jetait l'ancre dans le golfe saronique, voyageant sur les yachts d'Onassis ou de Sachs. Quant aux artistes, ils y trouvèrent l'inspiration : Leonard Cohen tomba amoureux à Hydra de la femme pour qui il écrira plus tard « So Long Marianne ». Un film de 1957 fut à l'origine de ces grands départs en vacances : « Ombres sous la mer » avec de splendides prises de vues de l'île et de la jeune Sophia Loren dans le rôle de Phèdre, une pêcheuse d'éponges. La pêche à l'éponge était autrefois une des plus importantes sources de revenus des hydriotes ; au milieu du XIXe siècle, la petite île comptait une des plus grandes fabriques d'éponges de la région. On peut encore visiter le bâtiment aujourd'hui et même y habiter, puisqu'il a été converti en hôtel de caractère. Le Bratsera Hotel tire son nom du « bratsera », le bateau sur lequel les plongeurs-pêcheurs d'éponges se reposaient. L'architecte Dimitris Papacharalampous a merveilleusement bien rénové le complexe, conféré au lobby une atmosphère de loft industriel et décoré les pièces avec du bois et des pierres de l'île (les chambres en mezzanine sont particulièrement réussies). Son style, conjuguant tradition et modernité, est simple et sophistiqué, naturel et glamour à la fois. Le Bratsera ferait un décor idéal pour un prochain film à Hydra.

Livres à emporter : « Flowers for Hitler » de Leonard Cohen.

ANREISE	Von Piräus aus erreicht man Hydra per Fähre in 1,5 Stunden. Die Insel ist autofrei, das Hotel liegt 2 Gehminuten vom Hafen entfernt.
PREISE	€€
ZIMMER	21 Zimmer, 5 Suiten.
KÜCHE	Auf der Karte des Restaurants stehen griechische und mediterrane Spezialitäten; im Sommer isst man auf der Veranda.
GESCHICHTE	Die Schwammfabrik wurde 1860 von Nickolaos Verneniotis erbaut, das Hotel eröffnete 1994.
X-FAKTOR	Der Pool und der blühende Garten sind Oasen.

ACCÈS	À partir du Pirée, on accède à Hydra en ferry en une heure et demie. Pas de voitures sur l'île, l'hôtel est à 2 min à pied du port.
PRIX	€€
CHAMBRES	21 chambres, 5 suites.
RESTAURATION	La carte du restaurant propose des spécialités grecques et méditerranénnes ; en été, on mange sur la terrasse.
HISTOIRE	La fabrique d'éponges a été édifiée en 1860 par Nickolaos Verneniotis, l'hôtel a ouvert ses portes en 1994.
LES « PLUS »	La piscine et le jardin fleuri sont de véritables oasis.

Modern Times
Orloff Resort, Spetses

Orloff Resort, Spetses

Modern Times

Spetses is for Athenians what Martha's Vineyard is for New Yorkers and the Île de Ré for Parisians: a beloved weekend destination and summer resort, an island with history and charm, beaches and marinas, as well as a place where spending relaxed days in a hotel or a private villa is more important than neon-lit nightlife. The island in the Argolic Gulf became famous after the Greek battle for independence against the Turks in 1821 – it was the home of the national heroine Laskarina Bouboulina, who sacrificed her entire fortune for the revolution. Those who wish to experience Spetses in an authentic and at the same time modern manner are best off in the Orloff Resort, opened by Christos Orloff and his two brothers in the garden of the former family seat – and not directly on the beach, but around a wonderful pool. The buildings in the style of the island are made of local materials; from the whitewashed walls of unpolished stone to the wooden-framed clay brick roofs. In the rooms the Orloffs unite geometrical strictness, simplicity and style – the minimalist ambience is offset by colours and designer chairs, such as Ron Arad's "Tom Vac". For families, the "Superior Residence" and the "Old Mansion" are ideal, each with its own kitchen and enough room for ten people. However, don't entrench yourself within your own four walls: otherwise you would miss the charm and charisma of your host, who likes to personally see to the wishes of his guests.
Book to pack: "The Magus" by John Fowles.

Orloff Resort

18050 Old Harbour

Spetses

Greece

Tel. +30 22980 75444

Fax +30 22980 74470

info@orloffresort.com

www.orloffresort.com

Open from the beginning of

April to the end of October

DIRECTIONS	Located near to the old harbour, 550 yards from Agia Marina beach. The transfer from Athens Airport is arranged (2–2 1/2-hour journey to Kosta, 5 min crossing).
RATES	€
ROOMS	11 rooms, 4 studios, 2 maisonettes, 2 villas.
FOOD	Breakfast is served in the hotel. A Greek restaurant is run by the Orloffs at the old harbour.
HISTORY	The family seat was built in 1865 (today the "Old Mansion"). The hotel, designed by Eliza Manola, has existed since 2004.
X-FACTOR	The veranda under ancient olive trees.

Moderne Zeiten

Spetses ist für die Athener das, was Martha's Vineyard für die New Yorker und die Île de Ré für die Pariser ist: Liebstes Wochenendziel und Sommerfrische, eine Insel mit Historie und Flair, Stränden und Jachthäfen sowie ein Ort, an dem entspannte Tage im Hotel oder in der eigenen Villa wichtiger sind als ein Nachtleben im Neonlicht. Die Insel im Argolischen Golf wurde nach dem griechischen Unabhängigkeitskampf gegen die Türken 1821 berühmt – war sie doch die Heimat der Nationalheldin Laskarina Bouboulina, die ihr ganzes Vermögen für die Revolution opferte. Wer Spetses authentisch und zeitgemäß zugleich erleben möchte, wohnt am besten im Orloff Resort, das Christos Orloff und seine beiden Brüder im Garten des ehemaligen Familiensitzes eröffnet haben – zwar nicht direkt am Strand gelegen, aber rund um einen wunderbaren Pool. Die Gebäude im Stil der Insel bestehen aus einheimischen Materialien; von den weiß getünchten Wänden aus ungeschliffenem Stein bis zu den holzgerahmten Lehmziegeldächern. In den Zimmern vereinen die Orloffs geometrische Strenge, Schlichtheit und Stil – aufgelockert wird das minimalistische Ambiente durch Farbakzente und Designerstühle wie Ron Arads »Tom Vac«. Ideal für Familien eignen sich die »Superior Residence« sowie die »Old Mansion« mit jeweils eigener Küche und Platz für zehn Personen. Verschanzen sollte man sich in den eigenen vier Wänden jedoch nicht, sonst entginge einem Charme und Charisma des Hausherren, der sich gerne persönlich um die Wünsche seiner Gäste kümmert.
Buchtipp: »Der Magus« von John Fowles.

Les temps modernes

Spetses est aux Athéniens ce que Martha's Vineyard est aux New-Yorkais et l'île de Ré aux Parisiens : une destination de prédilection pour les week-ends et les vacances, une île avec une histoire et du charme, des plages et des ports de plaisance ainsi qu'un endroit où des journées de détente à l'hôtel ou dans une villa ont plus d'importance qu'une vie nocturne agitée. Située dans le golfe Argolique, l'île est devenue célèbre après s'être brillamment illustrée dans la guerre d'indépendance contre les Turcs en 1821. Originaire de Spetses, Laskarina Bouboulina, une héroïne nationale, avait consacré toute sa fortune à la révolution qui conduira la Grèce à la victoire. Si vous voulez vivre la Spetses authentique et contemporaine, séjournez de préférence au Orloff Resort que Christos Orloff et ses deux frères ont ouvert dans le jardin de l'ancienne demeure familiale. Certes, il n'est pas directement au bord de la plage mais autour d'une magnifique piscine. Les bâtiments dans le style de l'île sont construits dans des matériaux locaux ; du badigeon blanc des murs en pierres brutes aux charpentes en bois et aux tuiles de brique. Dans les chambres, les Orloff ont réuni la rigueur géométrique, la simplicité et le style. Le caractère minimaliste est rompu par des touches de couleur et des chaises de designer comme les « Tom Vac » de Ron Arad. Idéales pour les familles la « Superior Residence » ainsi que la « Old Mansion » disposant d'une cuisine et de place pour 10 personnes. Toutefois, il serait dommage de se retrancher derrière ses murs et de ne pas profiter du charisme et du charme du maître des lieux qui s'occupe volontiers personnellement des désirs de ses hôtes.
Livre à emporter : « Le mage » de John Fowles.

ANREISE	Nahe des alten Hafens gelegen, 500 m vom Strand Agia Marina entfernt. Der Transfer vom Flughafen Athen wird arrangiert (2–2,5 Std. Fahrt nach Kostas, fünfminütige Überfahrt).
PREISE	€
ZIMMER	11 Zimmer, 4 Studios, 2 Maisonetten, 2 Villen.
KÜCHE	Im Hotel wird Frühstück serviert. Ein griechisches Restaurant führen die Orloffs am alten Hafen.
GESCHICHTE	1865 wurde der Familiensitz erbaut (heute die »Old Mansion«). Das von Eliza Manola entworfene Hotel besteht seit 2004.
X-FAKTOR	Die Veranda unter uralten Olivenbäumen.

ACCÈS	À proximité du vieux port, à 500 m de la plage Agia Marina. Transfert de l'aéroport d'Athènes organisé (2h–2 30 de trajet vers Kostas, puis traversée de 5 min en taxi de mer).
PRIX	€
CHAMBRES	11 chambres, 4 studios, 2 maisonnettes, 2 villas.
RESTAURATION	Petit déjeuner à l'hôtel. Les Orloff tiennent un restaurant grec au vieux port.
HISTOIRE	Cette propriété familiale a été construite en 1865 (de nos jours, le « Old Mansion »). L'hôtel conçu par l'architecte Eliza Manola a ouvert ses portes en 2004.
LES « PLUS »	La véranda sous les oliviers ancestraux.

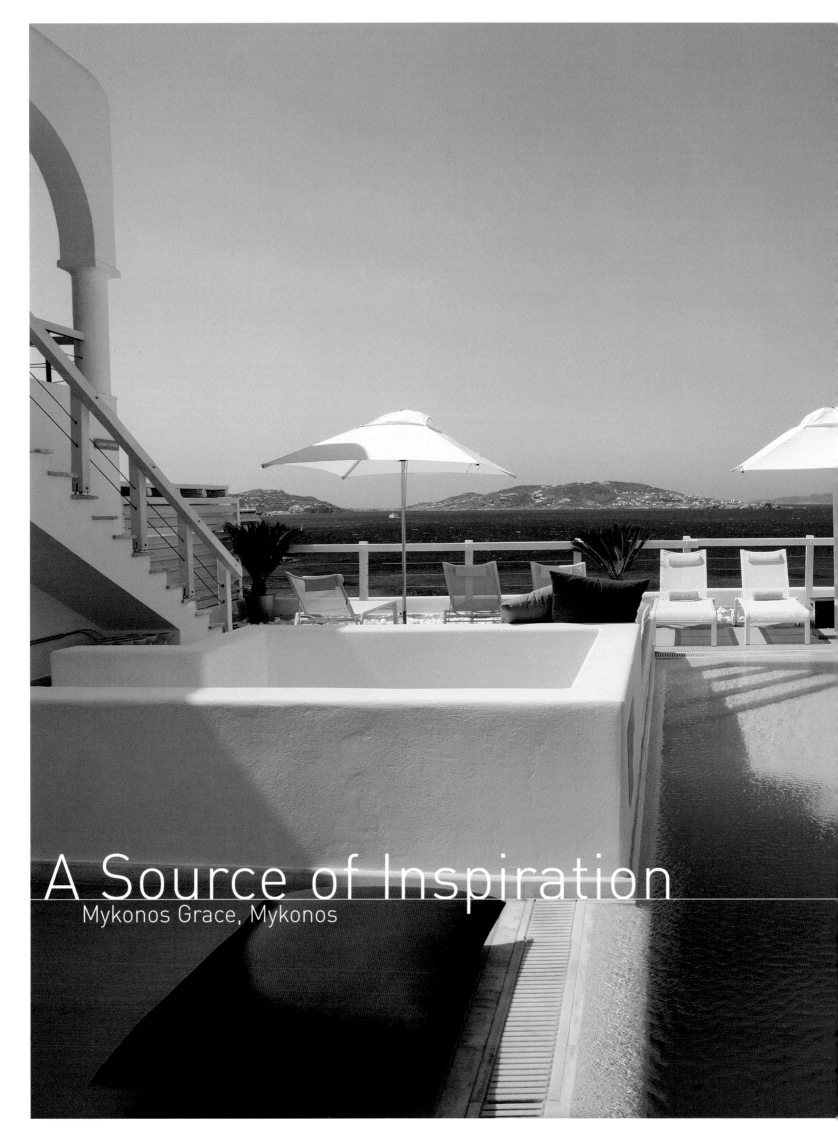

A Source of Inspiration

Mykonos Grace, Mykonos

Mykonos Grace, Mykonos

A Source of Inspiration

Those who have not seen the houses of Mykonos could not really claim to be an architect, Le Corbusier is said to have once stated. He and many of his colleagues took inspiration from the island's Cyclades architecture: from interlocking houses, erected to provide protection against heat, wind and at one time also pirates, with flat roofs and white walls as well as blue window frames, and from sacred buildings such as the Paraportiani Church, whose façade appears half Cubist, half biomorphic. Le Corbusier would probably cast a well-disposed glance at the Mykonos Grace Hotel today – it interprets the traditional style of the island in a modern way and has already won awards for just that. Situated above the sandy beach of Agios Stefanos and predominantly maintained in the classic colour combination of blue and white, its rooms afford panoramic views of the Aegean Sea. And the location provides insights into Greek mythology: opposite lies the island of Delos, birthplace of Apollo and site of one of the most important ritual places of antiquity. (Those who are not just amateur historians but also on their honeymoon should book the Honeymoon Suite on the top floor – it has a terrace with an olive tree and a particularly beautiful view.) What makes the hotel so very likeable is that it fits Mykonos not only in terms of its architecture. It has also picked up on the rhythm of the nocturnal island and serves breakfast into the evening.

Book to pack: "Travels in Greece" by Nikos Kazantzakis.

Mykonos Grace

Agios Stefanos

Mykonos 84600

Greece

Tel. +30 22890 20000

Fax +30 22890 26689

info@mykonosgrace.com

www.mykonosgrace.com

Open from the beginning of
April to mid-/the end of October

DIRECTIONS	Located north of the town of Mykonos. The airport is some 5 miles away.
RATES	€€
ROOMS	31 rooms.
FOOD	The "Grace Restaurant" serves Mediterranean dishes and has a bar.
HISTORY	Completely renovated by architects Dionysis Zacharias and Alexandra Stratou as well as by the design company Divercity, the hotel was opened in April 2007.
X-FACTOR	The pool and spa are perfect alternatives to the beach, which is a mere 5 min walk away.

Eine Quelle der Inspiration

Solange man die Häuser von Mykonos nicht gesehen habe, könne man nicht den Anspruch erheben, Architekt zu sein, soll Le Corbusier einmal gesagt haben. Er und viele seiner Kollegen ließen sich von der Kykladenarchitektur der Insel inspirieren: Von Häusern, die man zum Schutz gegen Hitze, Wind und einst auch Piraten ineinander verschachtelt errichtete, mit Flachdach und weißen Wänden sowie blauen Fensterrahmen ausstattete, und von Sakralbauten wie der Paraportiani-Kirche, deren Fassade halb kubistisch, halb biomorph anmutet. Le Corbusier würde auf das Mykonos Grace Hotel heute wahrscheinlich einen wohlwollenden Blick werfen – es interpretiert den traditionellen Stil der Insel modern und wurde dafür bereits preisgekrönt. Oberhalb des Sandstrands von Agios Stefanos gelegen und überwiegend in der klassischen Farbkombination Weiß-Blau gehalten, eröffnen seine Zimmer Panoramen über das Ägäische Meer sowie Einblicke in die griechische Mythologie: Gegenüber liegt die Insel Delos, auf der Apoll geboren wurde und die eine der wichtigsten Kultstätten der Antike war. Wer nicht nur Hobbyhistoriker, sondern auch auf Hochzeitsreise ist, sollte die »Honeymoon Suite« in der obersten Etage buchen – sie besitzt eine Terrasse mit Olivenbaum und besonders schöner Aussicht. Was das Hotel sehr sympathisch macht, ist, dass es nicht nur in puncto Architektur so gut nach Mykonos passt. Es hat auch den Rhythmus der nachtaktiven Insel aufgegriffen und serviert das Frühstück bis zum Abend.

Buchtipp: »Im Zauber der griechischen Landschaft« von Nikos Kazantzakis.

Une source d'inspiration

Le Corbusier aurait dit un jour que, tant que l'on a pas vu les maisons de Mykonos, on ne peut pas prétendre être architecte. Lui et de nombreux collègues se sont inspirés de l'architecture cycladique de l'île : des maisons imbriquées les unes dans les autres pour se protéger de la chaleur, du vent et jadis des pirates, aux toits plats, murs blancs chaulés et encadrements de fenêtres peints en bleu, ainsi que de bâtiments sacrés comme l'église Paraportiani, dont une moitié de la façade évoque le cubisme, l'autre montrant des formes organiques. Le Corbusier porterait probablement, de nos jours, un regard bienveillant sur le Mykonos Grace Hotel, déjà primé pour son architecture traditionnelle modernisée. Cet hôtel, essentiellement conçu dans les tons de bleu et blanc, se dresse au-dessus de la plage de sable d'Agios Stefanos. Depuis ses chambres, vous pourrez admirer un magnifique panorama sur la mer Egée et avoir même un aperçu de la mythologie grecque : l'île de Delos, sur laquelle Apollon est né et qui a joué un rôle considérable dans la Grèce antique, se trouve juste en face. Si vous êtes non seulement amateur d'histoire mais aussi en voyage de noces, réservez la suite « Honeymoon » au dernier étage. Elle possède une terrasse avec un olivier et une très belle vue. Ce qui rend le Mykonos Grace Hotel très sympathique, ce n'est pas seulement qu'il soit particulièrement en harmonie avec l'architecture de Mykonos, mais qu'il se soit également adapté aux nuits très animées sur l'île : on y sert le petit déjeuner jusqu'en soirée.

Livre à emporter : « Du Mont Sinaï à l'île de Venus. Carnet de voyage » de Nikos Kazantzakis.

ANREISE	Nördlich von Mykonos-Stadt gelegen. Der Flughafen ist 7 km entfernt.	ACCÈS	Au nord de la ville de Mykonos. L'aéroport est à 7 km.
PREISE	€€	PRIX	€€
ZIMMER	31 Zimmer.	CHAMBRES	31 chambres.
KÜCHE	Das »Grace Restaurant« serviert mediterrane Menüs und besitzt eine Bar.	RESTAURATION	Le « Grace Restaurant » sert une cuisine méditerranéenne et possède un bar.
GESCHICHTE	Das von den Architekten Dionysis Zacharias und Alexandra Stratou sowie von der Designfirma Divercity komplett umgebaute Hotel wurde im April 2007 eröffnet.	HISTOIRE	L'hôtel a été entièrement transformé par les architectes Dionysis Zacharias et Alexandra Stratou ainsi que par l'entreprise de design Divercity, puis il a ouvert ses portes en avril 2007.
X-FAKTOR	Pool und Spa sind perfekte Alternativen zum 5 Gehminuten entfernten Strand.	LES « PLUS »	La piscine et le spa sont d'excellentes alternatives à la plage qui se trouve à 5 min à pied.

...f knowing, the certainty of pr...
...f giving, the smile for no reason, t...
...t is yielding, the look that speaks vo...
...eep that is weightless, the release o...
...rust of fate, the patience of time, th...
...the certainty of right... gill nono x...

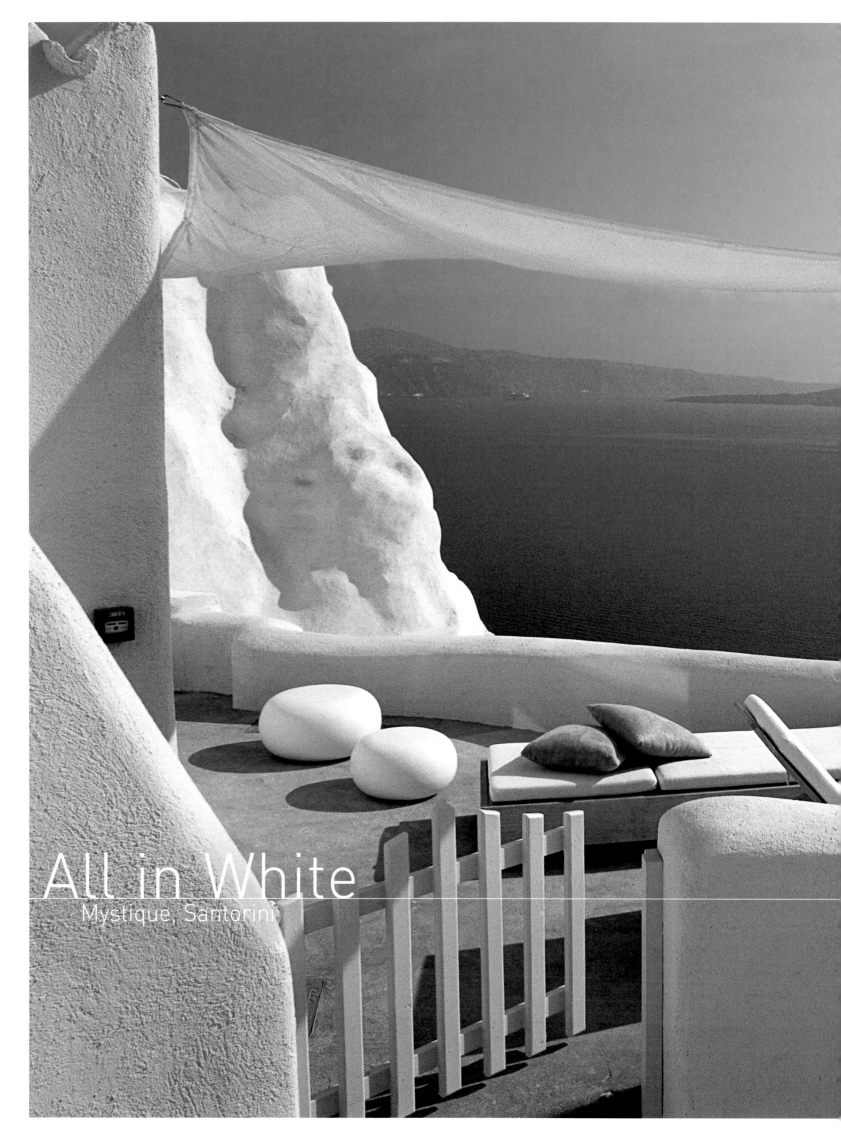

All in White
Mystique, Santorini

Mystique, Santorini

All in White

It is said to have been created from a lump of earth that was thrown into the sea from on board the "Argo". It was called Kalliste ("the most beautiful"), Thera ("the wild") and Strongyle ("the circular") – until one of the biggest volcanic eruptions of all time gave it its crescent shape. It inspires archaeologists to speculate if it was the Minoan culture or the legendary Atlantis that perished here: Santorini really cannot complain of a lack of history and stories. Many of them are told by the Caldera – the crater whose rocky walls plunge downwards a thousand feet deep into the Aegean and which is best marvelled at from the village of Oía. In its immediate vicinity, the Mystique has been built on a slope in the style typical of the country. However, only the shape of the suites recalls the traditional cave dwellings – everything else is light and luxurious. Frank Lefebvre has designed the rooms as a symphony in white and at the same time ensured that the interior does not leave a cool or aseptic impression: handmade driftwood furniture brings nature into the hotel; it is consciously plain and simple, unfinished and original – regulars affectionately describe the high-class ecological style as "Flintstone chic". Outside every room, a terrace covered with a canvas allows the interior and exterior worlds to merge into each other almost imperceptibly. In the daytime guests look out to sea from the veranda; at night they drink a glass of wine here by candlelight – and discover that Santorini is not merely myth, but also pure magic.

Book to pack: "The God of Impertinence" by Sten Nadolny.

Mystique Oía 84702 Santorini Greece Tel. +30 22860 71114 Fax +30 22860 71115 info@mystique.gr www.mystique.gr **Open from mid-April to the end of October**	

DIRECTIONS	Located in north Santorini, 11 miles southeast of the airport and some 13 miles from the harbour.
RATES	€€€€
ROOMS	18 suites, all with sea view.
FOOD	The "Charisma" restaurant is open to hotel guests only and serves modern Greek cuisine and selected wines in the open air. In addition there is a pool bar.
HISTORY	The hotel was opened in May 2007 and has already won several design prizes.
X-FACTOR	The infinity pool with a panoramic view.

Ganz in Weiß

Sie soll aus einem Klumpen Erde entstanden sein, der vom
Bord der »Argo« ins Meer geworfen wurde. Sie hieß Kalliste
(»Die Schönste«), Thera (»Die Wilde«) und Strongyle (»Die
Kreisrunde«) – so lange, bis ihr eine der größten Vulkan-
eruptionen aller Zeiten ihre sichelförmige Gestalt gab. Sie
lässt Archäologen spekulieren, ob hier die minoische Kultur
unterging oder das sagenumwobene Atlantis: Santorin kann
über einen Mangel an Geschichte und Geschichten wahrlich
nicht klagen. Viele von ihnen erzählt die Caldera – der
Krater, dessen Felswände bis zu 300 Meter tief in die Ägäis
abfallen und den man am besten vom Dorf Oía aus be-
staunt. Ganz in der Nähe wurde das Mystique im landes-
typischen Stil an den Hang gebaut. An die traditionellen
Höhlenwohnungen erinnert in den Suiten aber nur noch
die Form – alles andere ist licht, leicht und luxuriös. Frank
Lefebvre hat die runden Räume wie eine Sinfonie in Weiß
gestaltet und zugleich dafür gesorgt, dass das Interieur nicht
kühl oder aseptisch wirkt: Handgefertigte Möbel aus Treib-
holz bringen die Natur ins Haus; bewusst schlicht, unvoll-
kommen und ursprünglich – Stammgäste bezeichnen den
edlen Öko-Stil liebevoll auch als »Flintstone-Chic«. Eine mit
Segeltuch überspannte Terrasse vor jedem Zimmer lässt
Innen- und Außenwelt fast unmerklich ineinander überge-
hen. Von der Veranda aus blickt man tagsüber weit übers
Meer und trinkt abends ein Glas Wein im Kerzenschein –
und entdeckt, dass Santorin nicht nur ein Mythos ist,
sondern auch pure Magie.

**Buchtipps: »Ein Gott der Frechheit« von Sten Nadolny, »Die
griechischen Landschaften« und »Das Ägäische Meer und seine
Inseln« von Alfred Philippson.**

Symphonie de blanc

Selon la légende, elle serait née d'une motte de terre jetée
dans la mer depuis le navire « Argo ». Elle s'appela Kallisté
(« la très belle »), Théra (« la sauvage ») et Strongylé (« la
ronde ») jusqu'au jour où une des plus grandes éruptions
volcaniques de tous les temps lui donna sa forme de faucille.
Les archéologues pensent qu'elle aurait causé la disparition
de la civilisation minoenne et, par conséquent, de la légendaire
Atlantide. Santorin peut donc s'enorgueillir de son histoire
et de ses nombreuses légendes. Beaucoup sont racontées par
la Caldera, ce cratère dont les parois sombrent dans la mer
Egée jusqu'à 300 mètres de profondeur et que l'on peut le
mieux admirer depuis le village d'Oía. Non loin de là, vous
trouverez le Mystique construit à flanc de falaise dans le
style typique de l'île. Ses suites n'ont gardé des logements
troglodytiques traditionnels que la forme, le reste n'est que
lumière, légèreté et luxe. Frank Lefebvre a aménagé ces
pièces rondes dans une symphonie de blanc tout en veillant
à ce que l'intérieur ne paraisse pas froid ni stérile. Le mobilier artisanal en bois flottant fait rentrer la nature dans la
maison ; tout est voulu simple, naturel et authentique. Les
habitués qualifient gentiment ce style écolo-chic de « chic
à la Flintstone ». Chaque chambre comprend une terrasse
couvert d'une toile à voile qui fait le lien entre l'intérieur et
l'extérieur. De la véranda, vous aurez dans la journée une
vue imprenable sur la mer. Le soir, vous y prendrez un verre
à la lueur de bougies et vous découvrirez que Santorin n'est
pas seulement un mythe, mais aussi pure magie.

Livre à emporter : « Hermès l'insolent » de Sten Nadolny.

ANREISE	Im Norden Santorins gelegen, 18 km südöstlich vom Flughafen und 20 km vom Hafen entfernt.
PREISE	€€€€
ZIMMER	18 Suiten, alle mit Meerblick.
KÜCHE	Das Restaurant »Charisma« steht nur Hotelgästen offen und serviert unter freiem Himmel moderne griechische Menüs und ausgesuchte Weine. Zudem gibt es eine Poolbar.
GESCHICHTE	Das Hotel wurde im Mai 2007 eröffnet und gewann bereits mehrere Designpreise.
X-FAKTOR	Der randlose Pool mit Panoramablick.

ACCÈS	Au nord de Santorin, à 18 km au sud-est de l'aéroport et à 20 km du port.
PRIX	€€€€
CHAMBRES	18 suites, toutes avec vue sur la mer.
RESTAURATION	Le restaurant « Charisma » est réservé aux clients de l'hôtel. il sert une cuisine grecque moderne et des vins de premier choix en plein air. Il y a aussi un pool-bar.
HISTOIRE	L'hôtel a ouvert ses portes en mai 2007 et a déjà rem- porté de nombreux prix de design.
LES « PLUS »	La piscine à débordement avec vue panoramique.

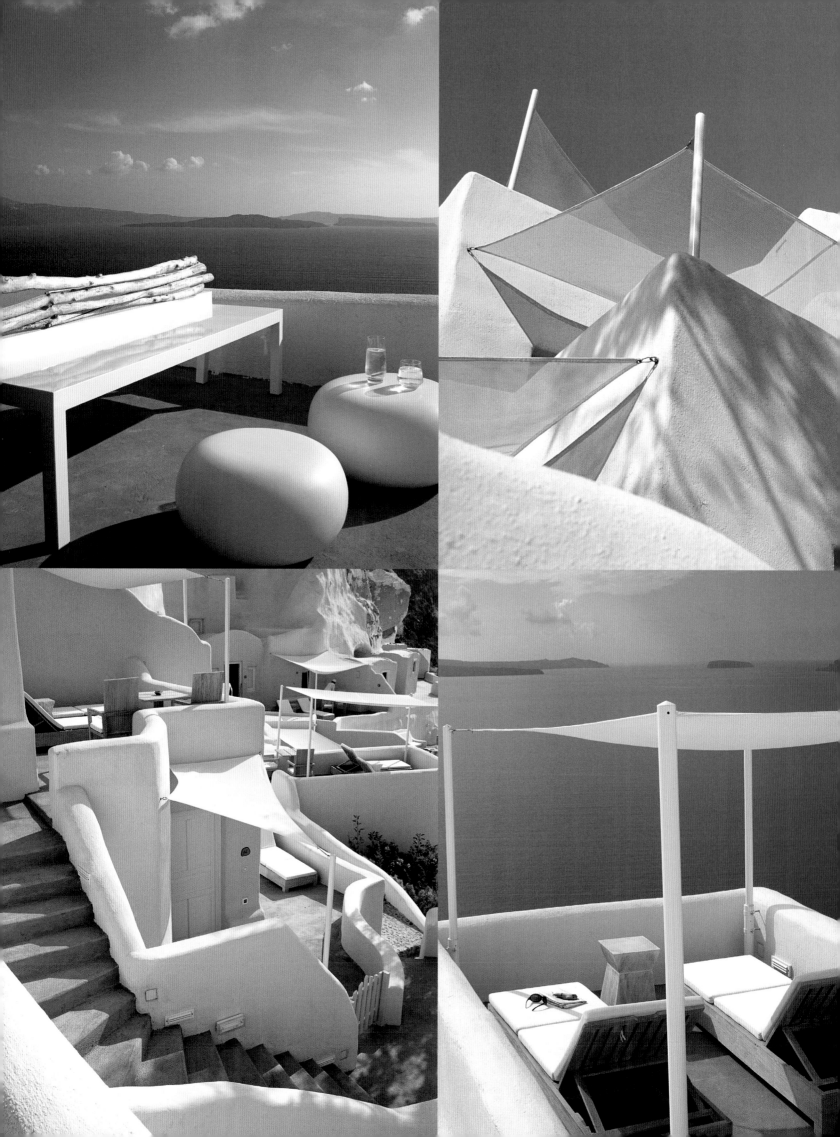

New Horizons
Perivolas, Santorini

Perivolas, Santorini

New Horizons

The star of Santorini is the sunset. On clear summer evenings it delivers a show of superlatives, a play of colours in pink, violet and blue, at the end of which the sun, an orange-red fireball, sinks into the black, shimmering Aegean and is extinguished. A beautiful, romantic spectacle, fit for the silver screen – one that unfortunately must be shared with countless other admirers who set up their cameras, tripod alongside tripod, on the rim of the crater or compete for the most desirable spots in bars that advertise themselves by claiming the "best view" on the island. But there is one exception: those lucky enough to be able to stay in Perivolas enjoy the sunset exclusively from their own private veranda. Once, fishermen and farmers lived in these cave-like houses, built into the vineyard on slopes of soft lava rock that extend like an amphitheatre to a central terrace. Costis Psychas and his parents have transformed the caves into hideaways – with vaulted, whitewashed ceilings, furniture manufactured on the island and colourful fabrics. The two "Perivolas Suites" even offer the luxury of their own pool; these are situated less spectacularly, however, than the rimless main pool, which seems to flow directly into the Aegean. The restaurant, which in the evenings serves Mediterranean dishes exclusively for guests, is right next to the pool. Dinner is eaten by candlelight – and naturally only after sunset, when Santorini's star has completed its performance.

Book to pack: "The Colossus of Maroussi" by Henry Miller.

Perivolas
Oía 84702
Santorini
Greece
Tel. +30 22860 71308
Fax +30 22860 71309
info@perivolas.gr
www.perivolas.gr
Open from April to October

DIRECTIONS	Located near Oía, 30 min from the airport, 40 min from Santorini harbour. There is no private beach.
RATES	€€€
ROOMS	20 private houses; depending on category between 270 and 1500 square feet in size. All with private terrace.
FOOD	The restaurant has been created in a former wine cellar.
HISTORY	The cave dwellings were built more than 300 years ago. The hotel project started in the 1960s and was completed in the middle of the first decade of this century.
X-FACTOR	The unusually obliging service.

Neue Horizonte

Der Star von Santorin ist der Sonnenuntergang. Er liefert an klaren Sommerabenden eine Show der Superlative, ein Farbenspiel in Rosa, Violett und Blau, an dessen Ende die Sonne wie ein orangeroter Feuerball in die schwarz schimmernde Ägäis abtaucht und erlischt. Ein wunderschönes, leinwandtaugliches und romantisches Schauspiel – das man nur leider mit ungezählten anderen Bewunderern teilen muss, die am Kraterrand ihre Fotoapparate Stativ an Stativ aufbauen oder um die begehrtesten Plätze in Bars kämpfen, die mit dem »besten Blick« der Insel werben. Eine Ausnahme gibt es jedoch: Wer das Glück hat, im Perivolas wohnen zu können, genießt den Sonnenuntergang exklusiv von seiner privaten Veranda aus. Einst lebten Fischer und Bauern in diesen höhlenartigen Häusern, die in den Weinberg aus weichem Lavagestein gebaut worden waren, der sich wie ein Amphitheater zu einer zentralen Terrasse zieht. Costis Psychas und seine Eltern haben die Höhlen in Hideaways verwandelt – mit gewölbten, weiß getünchten Decken, auf der Insel gefertigten Möbeln sowie bunten Stoffen. Die zwei »Perivolas«-Suiten bieten sogar den Luxus eigener Pools; diese liegen aber nicht ganz so spektakulär wie der randlose Hauptpool, der direkt in die Ägäis zu fließen scheint. Gleich neben dem Becken befindet sich das Restaurant, das abends ausschließlich für Hotelgäste mediterrane Menüs serviert. Gegessen wird im Kerzenschein – und natürlich erst nach Sonnenuntergang, wenn Santorins Star seinen Auftritt hatte.

Buchtipp: »Der Koloss von Maroussi« von Henry Miller.

De nouveaux horizons

A Santorin, le coucher du soleil est un rendez-vous à ne pas manquer. C'est une vraie féerie de couleurs en rose, violet et bleu qui vous attend les soirs d'été par temps clair. Au final le soleil plonge, tel une boule de feu, dans la mer Egée aux reflets noirs et s'éteint. Un spectacle éblouissant, pittoresque et romantique qu'il faut malheureusement partager avec d'innombrables admirateurs, tous ayant installé les trépieds de leurs appareils photo les uns à côté des autres au bord du cratère ou luttant pour avoir les meilleures places dans les bars qui promettent la « plus belle vue » de l'île. Il existe toutefois une exception : si vous avez la chance de pouvoir séjourner au Perivolas, vous pourrez profiter du coucher de soleil en exclusivité depuis votre terrasse privée. Ces demeures troglodytiques, construites dans de la pierre ponce, se trouvaient autrefois dans des vignobles aménagés en amphithéâtre, et étaient habitées par des pêcheurs et des paysans. Costis Psychas et ses parents ont transformé ces maisons en refuges aux plafonds voûtés et blanchis à la chaux, aux meubles de fabrication locale et aux tissus colorés. Les deux suites « Perivolas » offrent même le luxe de piscines privées ; toutefois, elles sont moins spectaculaires que la grande piscine à débordement qui semble se déverser directement dans la mer Egée. Le restaurant se trouve juste à côté du bassin. Une cuisine méditerranéenne y est servie en soirée, uniquement pour les clients de l'hôtel. Vous dînerez aux chandelles, après avoir observé le coucher du soleil en privilégié, évidemment.

Livre à emporter : « Le colosse de Maroussi » d'Henry Miller.

ANREISE	Bei Oía gelegen, 30 min vom Flughafen, 40 min vom Hafen Santorin entfernt. Ein eigener Strand ist nicht vorhanden.
PREISE	€€€
ZIMMER	20 private Häuser; je nach Kategorie zwischen 25 und 140 qm groß. Alle mit privater Terrasse.
KÜCHE	Das Restaurant entstand in einer ehemaligen Weinkellerei.
GESCHICHTE	Die Höhlenwohnungen wurden vor mehr als 300 Jahren gebaut. Das Hotelprojekt startete in den 1960ern und wurde Mitte der 2000er-Jahre fertiggestellt.
X-FAKTOR	Der außergewöhnlich zuvorkommende Service.

ACCÈS	À Oía, à 30 min de l'aéroport, à 40 min du port de Santorin. Pas de plage.
PRIX	€€€
CHAMBRES	20 habitations privées ; entre 25 et 140 m² selon le prix. Toutes avec une terrasse privée.
RESTAURATION	Le restaurant est situé dans une ancienne cave à vins.
HISTOIRE	Les demeures troglodytiques ont été construites il y a plus de 300 ans. Le projet hôtelier a débuté dans les années 1960 et s'est achevé au milieu de l'année 2000.
LES « PLUS »	Un service extrêmement attentionné.

With the Greatest Pleasure
Katikies, Santorini

Katikies, Santorini

With the Greatest Pleasure

It shines orange-gold in the glass, has the soft aroma of honey, and on the palate notes of apricot and fig unfold: Vinsanto is Santorini's most famous white wine. Its name simply indicates its origins (this "wine from Santorini" is no "holy wine", as is sometimes claimed), and its grapes grow on terraces thousands of years old. They draw their special taste from the volcanic soil, and are pressed only after having been dried in the sun. For at least two years the Vinsanto matures in oak barrels, before it is served well chilled – ideally to accompany strong cheese and most stylishly of all in the Katikies on Santorini itself. Every evening, the boutique hotel high above the caldera invites guests to wine tastings; precisely at the time when the sunset provides the island with its loveliest play of colours. It is hard to believe that this pleasure can be heightened still further – but the Katikies makes that possible, because it is in possession of the most romantic dinner restaurant of the Cyclades: situated on an intimate rooftop terrace with only four tables that are subtly lit and from which there is a million-dollar view onto the night-time Aegean. The hotel is a feast for the eyes in the daytime, too, when it shows itself off in gleaming white and presents architecture that combines Santorini's traditional style with imaginative modern forms. Those who are happy to negotiate the steps are best off in the elegant suites up on the slope – with private verandas and a postcard panorama over Santorini, the island of Vinsanto.

Book to pack: "The Plant, the Well, the Angel: A Trilogy" by Vassilis Vassilikos.

Katikies	
Oía 84702	
Santorini	
Greece	
Tel. +30 22860 71401	
Fax +30 22860 71129	
info@katikies.com	
www.katikieshotelsantorini.com	
Open from the beginning of	
April to the end of November	

DIRECTIONS	Located in Oía, 11 miles from Santorini's airport and harbour.
RATES	€€€
ROOMS	27 rooms and suites.
FOOD	Both the "Katikies Dinner Restaurant" and the "Pool Restaurant Kirini" serve first-class Mediterranean cuisine. In addition there is a pool bar.
HISTORY	The Katikies is considered the Grande Dame of the island's hotel business; it was opened in 1986 and renovated in 2004.
X-FACTOR	The rimless pools, whose blue merges with that of the sky and the sea.

Genuss auf höchstem Niveau

Er glänzt orange-golden im Glas, duftet zart nach Honig
und entfaltet am Gaumen ein Aroma von Aprikose und Feige:
Der Vinsanto ist der berühmteste Weißwein von Santorin.
Sein Name bezeichnet ganz einfach seine Herkunft (der
»Wein aus Santorin« ist kein »heiliger Wein«, wie manchmal behauptet wird), und seine Trauben wachsen auf jahr-
tausendealten Terrassen. Die Früchte ziehen ihren besonderen
Geschmack aus dem Vulkanboden, ehe sie in der Sonne
getrocknet und erst dann gekeltert werden. Mindestens
zwei Jahre reift der Vinsanto in Eichenfässern, ehe er gut
gekühlt serviert wird – am besten zu intensivem Käse
und am stilvollsten auf Santorin selbst, im Katikies. Das
Boutiquehotel hoch über der Caldera lädt jeden Abend zur
Weinverkostung – genau dann, wenn die Sonne untergeht
und der Insel ihr schönstes Farbenspiel bereitet. Es ist
schwer zu glauben, dass sich dieser Genuss noch steigern
lässt – doch es ist möglich, denn das Katikies besitzt das
romantischste Dinnerrestaurant der Kykladen: Auf einer
intimen Dachterrasse gelegen, umfasst es nur vier Tische,
die dezent beleuchtet werden und einen Millionen-Dollar-
Blick auf die nächtliche Ägäis eröffnen. Ein Augenschmaus
ist das Hotel aber auch tagsüber, denn dann zeigt es sich in
strahlendem Weiß und präsentiert eine Architektur, die den
traditionellen Stil Santorins mit modernen Fantasieformen
verbindet. Wer Treppen nicht scheut, wohnt am schönsten
in den eleganten Suiten ganz oben am Hang – mit privaten
Verandas und Postkartenpanorama über Santorin, die Insel
des Vinsanto.

Buchtipp: »Griechische Trilogie« von Vassilis Vassilikos.

Un goût incomparable

De couleur ambrée, il dégage une douce odeur de miel et
développe des arômes d'abricot et de figue : le vinsanto est le
vin doux le plus célèbre de Santorin. Son nom désigne tout
simplement son origine (vinsanto signifie « vin de Santorin »,
et non « vin saint » comme on pourrait le croire). Les raisins
du vinsanto poussent sur des terrasses millénaires et tirent
leur goût particulier du sol volcanique, avant qu'ils ne soient
séchés au soleil puis pressés. Le vin est ensuite élevé en fûts
de chêne pendant au moins deux ans, avant d'être bu très frais
en accompagnement d'un fromage bien fait par exemple,
idéalement sur place à Santorin, au Katikies. Cet hôtel boutique, qui domine la caldeira, invite tous les soirs à la dégustation de vins ; au moment où le soleil se couche et où l'île
prépare son plus beau jeu de couleurs. Difficile de croire
que ce plaisir peut être encore sublimé. Mais c'est possible,
car le Katikies possède le restaurant le plus romantique des
Cyclades : seulement quatre tables sur une terrasse intimiste,
éclairées à la bougie, avec une vue qui n'a pas de prix sur
la mer Egée de nuit. Mais cet hôtel est également un festin
pour les yeux dans la journée : son architecture blanche
éclatante allie le style traditionnel de Santorin à des formes
modernes. Si vous ne craignez pas de grimper des marches,
les suites les plus élégantes sont tout en haut de la colline.
Elles sont toutes dotées de terrasses privées offrant un panorama de carte postale sur Santorin, l'île du vinsanto.

**Livre à emporter : « Trilogie : la plante, le puits, l'ange »
de Vassilis Vassilikos.**

ANREISE	In Oía gelegen, 18 km vom Flughafen und Hafen Santorins entfernt.
PREISE	€€€
ZIMMER	27 Zimmer und Suiten.
KÜCHE	Sowohl das »Katikies Dinner Restaurant« als auch das »Pool Restaurant Kirini« servieren erstklassige mediter-rane Küche. Zudem gibt es eine Poolbar.
GESCHICHTE	Das Katikies gilt als Grande Dame der Inselhotellerie, es wurde 1986 eröffnet und 2004 renoviert.
X-FAKTOR	Die randlosen Pools, deren Blau mit dem von Himmel und Meer zusammenfließt.

ACCÈS	À Oía, à 18 km de l'aéroport et du port de Santorin.
PRIX	€€€
CHAMBRES	27 chambres et suites.
RESTAURATION	Excellente cuisine méditerranéenne aussi bien au « Katikies Dinner Restaurant » qu'au « Pool Restaurant Kirini ». Il existe aussi un bar au bord de la piscine.
HISTOIRE	Le Katikies est le nec plus ultra de l'hôtellerie sur l'île, il a ouvert ses portes en 1986 et a été rénové en 2004.
LES « PLUS »	Les piscines à débordement dont le bleu se fond dans celui du ciel et de la mer.

Hidden on the Coast
The Old Phoenix, Crete

The Old Phoenix, Crete

Hidden on the Coast

Crete's coastline is well over 600 miles long – the most spectacular stretches are along the island's south coast. Here, the cliffs are steep, rough and furrowed, and the White Mountains are cut through with canyons such as the legendary Samaria Gorge. It made history in the 19th century as a hiding place for Cretan members of the resistance against the Turks (the rebels even set up a printing works there in order to be able to print newspapers), and when the German Wehrmacht attacked Crete in 1941 the gorge served as an escape route to the sea for the King of Greece and his prime minister. Admittedly its fame makes the Samaria Gorge a magnet for visitors: in the high season hoards of people hike across the rock faces; after a tour like this, those who prefer their own company are in urgent need not only of a breather, but also of silence and solitude. They find all that in the nearby bay of Finix, only accessible by boat, in which The Old Phoenix hotel stands. The rooms in the white buildings with blue shutters are furnished very simply, on the principle of "bed-cupboard-table"; but who needs an opulent interior when you have a balcony with a breathtaking view onto the Libyan Sea? There is a fabulous view, too, from the terrace, on which down-to-earth meals are served: the fish is caught by the hotel staff themselves and the cheese comes from the hotel's own goats and sheep. The pebble beach is the best place for a siesta – alone under the parasol and far removed from the hustle and bustle on Crete's coast.

Book to pack: "Zorba the Greek" by Nikos Kazantzakis.

The Old Phoenix
Finikas, Sfakion
73013 Crete
Greece
Tel./Fax +30 282 509 1257 and +30 282 509 1126
info@old-phoenix.com
www.old-phonix.com
**Open from the end of April
to the end of October**

DIRECTIONS	Travel by car to Hora Sfakion (47 miles from Chania Airport, 99 miles from Heraklion Airport) and take the 15-20-min ferry ride to Loutro; the hotel is reached after a 15-min walk.
RATES	€
ROOMS	28 rooms.
FOOD	Mainly local products are used for the traditional dishes on offer here.
HISTORY	The hotel has been run by the Athitakis family since its opening in 1978.
X-FACTOR	The enchanting little church just above the hotel.

An der Küste versteckt

Kretas Küstenlinie ist mehr als 1000 Kilometer lang – die spektakulärsten von ihnen ziehen sich am Südrand der Insel entlang. Dort sind die Felsen steil, rau und zerfurcht, und durch die Weißen Berge schneiden Canyons wie die legendäre Samaria-Schlucht. Sie schrieb im 19. Jahrhundert als Versteck kretischer Widerstandskämpfer gegen die Türken Geschichte (die Rebellen richteten dort sogar eine Druckerei ein, um eigene Zeitungen herstellen zu können), und als die deutsche Wehrmacht 1941 Kreta überfiel, diente die Schlucht dem griechischen König und seinem Ministerpräsidenten als Fluchtweg zum Meer. Ihre Berühmtheit macht die Samaria-Schlucht freilich zum Besuchermagnet: Zur Hochsaison wandern täglich Scharen an den Felswänden entlang; Einzelgänger brauchen nach der Tour dringend eine Verschnaufpause, Ruhe und Einsamkeit. All das finden sie in der nahen Bucht von Finix, die nur per Boot erreichbar ist und in der das Hotel The Old Phoenix steht. Die Zimmer in den weißen Gebäuden mit blauen Fensterläden sind sehr schlicht nach dem Prinzip »Bett-Schrank-Tisch« eingerichtet; aber wer benötigt ein opulenteres Interieur, wenn er draußen einen eigenen Balkon mit atemberaubendem Blick aufs Libysche Meer besitzt? Sagenhaft ist die Sicht auch von der Terrasse aus, auf der eine bodenständige Küche serviert wird: Der Fisch ist selbst gefangen, und der Käse stammt von den hoteleigenen Ziegen und Schafen. Siesta hält man besten am Kieselstrand – alleine unterm Sonnenschirm und weit entfernt vom Trubel an Kretas Küste.
Buchtipp: »Alexis Sorbas« von Nikos Kazantzakis.

Dissimulé sur la côte

La Crète a plus de 1 000 kilomètres de côtes, et c'est dans le sud de l'île que s'étendent les plus spectaculaires. Les rochers y sont escarpés et fissurés, des canyons, se taillent un passage à travers les Montagnes Blanches, comme les légendaires gorges de Samaria. Elles jouèrent un rôle important dans l'histoire du XIXe siècle en servant de cachette aux résistants crétois qui combattaient l'invasion turque (les rebelles y aménagèrent même une imprimerie pour pouvoir fabriquer leurs propres journaux), et lorsque la Wehrmacht allemande envahit la Crète en 1941, le roi de Grèce et son Premier ministre s'enfuirent à travers les gorges pour rejoindre la mer. Les gorges de Samaria jouissent d'une telle célébrité qu'elles attirent une foule de visiteurs. En haute saison, des hordes de randonneurs arpentent les passages ; les promeneurs solitaires auront, eux, un grand besoin de calme et de solitude pour se ressourcer. C'est tout ce que propose la baie de Finix à proximité, accessible uniquement par bateau et où se trouve l'hôtel The Old Phoenix. Les chambres, dans ces bâtiments blancs aux volets bleus, sont aménagées très simplement d'après le principe « lit-table-armoire ». Mais n'est-ce pas suffisant quand on dispose à l'extérieur d'un balcon avec un panorama à couper le souffle sur la mer de Libye ? La terrasse bénéficie également d'une vue fabuleuse. On y sert une cuisine rustique : le poisson est pêché sur place et le fromage est fait à partir du lait des chèvres et brebis de l'hôtel. L'endroit idéal pour faire la sieste est la plage de galets, seul sous votre parasol et loin du tumulte des côtes de la Crète.
Livre à emporter : « Alexis Zorba » de Nikos Kazantzakis.

ANREISE	Man fährt mit dem Auto nach Hora Sfakion (75 km vom Flughafen Chania, 160 km vom Flughafen Heraklion entfernt), setzt in 15-20 min mit der Fähre nach Loutro über und erreicht das Hotel nach 15 Gehminuten.
PREISE	€
ZIMMER	28 Zimmer.
KÜCHE	Für die traditionellen Menüs werden hauptsächlich lokale Produkte verwendet.
GESCHICHTE	Das Hotel wird seit seiner Eröffnung 1978 von der Familie Athitakis geführt.
X-FAKTOR	Die zauberhafte kleine Kirche gleich oberhalb des Hotels.

ACCÈS	Se rendre en voiture jusqu'à Hora Sfakion (à 75 km de l'aéroport de Chania, à 160 km de l'aéroport d'Héraklion), faire la traversée en bateau de 15-20 min en direction de Loutro puis marcher 15 min à pied jusqu'à l'hôtel.
PRIX	€
CHAMBRES	28 chambres.
RESTAURATION	Cuisine traditionnelle à base de produits principalement régionaux.
HISTOIRE	L'hôtel est dirigé par la famille Athitakis depuis son ouverture en 1978.
LES « PLUS »	La ravissante petite église juste au-dessus de l'hôtel.

FULL BREAKFAST

GREECE · CAFE · NESCAFE
TEA · MOUNTAIN · TEA
fresh joghurt with
mountain honey
fresh fruit salad
fresh orange juice
toast with ham + cheese
eggs boiled or fried or with ham
special omelette
sfakia pita (traditional)
DIFFERENT KINDS OF TRADITIONAL CHEESE

A Real Gem
Mehmet Ali Ağa Mansion, Datça

Mehmet Ali Ağa Mansion, Datça

A Real Gem

When this Anatolian manor house was built for the influential Tuhfezade family at the beginning of the 19th century, it was the first building in the region to have glass windows – and it was so spacious that the locals respectfully dubbed it "koca ev", large house. For 200 years it was among the most magnificent buildings on the Datça Peninsula – however it fell into disrepair when the Tuhfezades died out, and was used by its new owners only as a tobacco store, a cinema and a school. It is thanks to Mehmet Pir that today it is an atmospheric hotel and at the same time a museum that tells of the art and culture of southwestern Turkey. He restored the property true to the original, repaired original stones and cedarwood on site and reassembled the material according to traditional methods – including the use of handmade nails and dowels. From the former parlour, Pir made the most breathtaking suite in the hotel – with original frescoes depicting exotic animals and flowers, as well as a richly decorated ceiling, in the middle of which a wheel of fortune spins, symbolising eternity. The other rooms in the mansion are named after the legendary Seven Sleepers and furnished with French and English antiques; alternatively guests can stay in the new annexes, whose rooms offer a modern take on old Ottoman style. The splendid hammam and the hotel's own library with books on the history of the region fit the concept perfectly – and in this way the era of the Tuhfezades is brought back to life.

Book to pack: "The New Life" by Orhan Pamuk.

Mehmet Ali Ağa Mansion

Reşadiye Mah. Kavak Meydanı

48900 Datça – Muğla

Turkey

Tel. +90 252 7129 257

Fax +90 252 7129 256

info@kocaev.com

www.kocaev.com

Open from the beginning of May to the end of October

DIRECTIONS	Situated on a hill near Datça in the middle of a lovely garden. The easiest way to reach the peninsula is by ferry from Bodrum (2 1/2 hrs).
RATES	€€
ROOMS	4 rooms, 1 suite in the main building; 12 rooms, 1 suite in the annexes.
FOOD	In the "Elaki Restaurant" old Anatolian recipes are given a modern touch; in addition there is a traditional café and a wine cellar.
HISTORY	The hotel was opened in 2004.
X-FACTOR	The private beach is 2 1/2 miles away.

Ein Schmuckstück

Als dieses anatolische Herrenhaus Anfang des 19. Jahrhunderts für die einflussreiche Familie Tuhfezade errichtet wurde, war es das erste Gebäude der Region, das Glasfenster besaß – und so weitläufig, dass die Einheimischen es respektvoll »koca ev«, »großes Haus«, nannten. 200 Jahre lang zählte es zu den prachtvollsten Bauten auf der Datça-Halbinsel – verlor seinen Glanz aber mit dem Aussterben der Tuhfezades und wurde von neuen Besitzern nur noch als Tabaklager, Kino sowie Schule genutzt. Dass es heute ein Hotel mit Atmosphäre ist und zugleich ein Museum, das von Kunst und Kultur der Südwesttürkei erzählt, ist Mehmet Pir zu verdanken. Er erneuerte das Anwesen originalgetreu, restaurierte ursprünglich verwendete Steine und Zedernholz direkt vor Ort und setzte das Material nach traditionellen Methoden wieder zusammen – unter anderem mit handgefertigten Nägeln und Dübeln. Aus dem ehemaligen Salon machte Pir die atemberaubendste Suite des Hauses – mit antiken Fresken, die exotische Tiere und Blumen zeigen, sowie einer reich verzierten Decke, in deren Mitte sich ein Glücksrad dreht und die Ewigkeit symbolisiert. Die weiteren Zimmer der Mansion sind nach den legendären Sieben Schläfern benannt und mit französischen und englischen Antiquitäten eingerichtet; alternativ kann man auch in den neuen Nebengebäuden wohnen, deren Räume den alten ottomanischen Stil modern interpretieren. Perfekt ins Konzept passen der herrliche Hamam und die hauseigene Bibliothek mit Titeln zur Geschichte der Gegend – so lebt die vergangene Ära der Tuhfezades wieder auf.

Buchtipp: »Das neue Leben« von Orhan Pamuk.

Un bijou

Ce manoir anatolien fut édifié au début du XIXᵉ siècle pour une famille influente, les Tuhfezade. Il était le premier bâtiment de la région à posséder de grandes fenêtres vitrées et si vaste que les autochtones le surnommèrent respectueusement « koca ev », la grande maison. Il fut pendant 200 ans l'une des plus belles constructions de la presqu'île de Datça, mais il perdit de son éclat avec l'extinction de la famille Tuhfezade et fut ensuite utilisé comme entrepôt de tabac, cinéma et école. L'actuel hôtel et musée, relatant l'art et la culture de la Turquie du sud-ouest, est l'œuvre de Mehmet Pir. Il restaura la propriété en restant fidèle à l'original, réhabilita directement sur place les pierres et le cèdre d'origine et assembla les matériaux selon des méthodes traditionnelles, avec entre autres des clous et des goujons fait main. Pir fit de l'ancien salon la suite la plus grandiose de la maison. Elle arbore des fresques anciennes montrant des animaux et des fleurs exotiques et un plafond richement décoré comprenant en son centre une roue de la fortune, symbole de l'éternité. Les autres chambres de ce manoir portent le nom des légendaires Septs Dormants et sont aménagées avec des antiquités françaises et anglaises ; mais il est également possible d'habiter dans les nouvelles annexes dont les pièces ont été décorées dans un style ottoman modernisé. Le magnifique hammam et la bibliothèque abritant des ouvrages sur l'histoire des environs sont en parfaite harmonie avec ce concept : ainsi renaît l'ère des Tuhfezade.

Livre à emporter : « La vie nouvelle » d'Orhan Pamuk.

ANREISE	Auf einem Hügel bei Datça inmitten schöner Gärten gelegen. Am einfachsten erreicht man die Halbinsel per Fähre ab Bodrum (2,5 Stunden).
PREISE	€€
ZIMMER	4 Zimmer, 1 Suite im Haupthaus; 12 Zimmer, 1 Suite in den Nebengebäuden.
KÜCHE	Im »Elaki Restaurant« erhalten alte anatolische Rezepte einen modernen Touch; zudem gibt es ein traditionelles Café und einen Weinkeller.
GESCHICHTE	Das Hotel wurde 2004 eröffnet.
X-FAKTOR	Der private Strand ist 4 km entfernt.

ACCÈS	Sur une colline non loin de Datça, au milieu de beaux jardins. Pour atteindre la péninsule plus facilement, faites la traversée en ferry (2h 30) à partir de Bodrum.
PRIX	€€
CHAMBRES	4 chambres, 1 suite dans le bâtiment principal ; 12 chambres, 1 suite dans les annexes.
RESTAURATION	L' « Elaki Restaurant » propose des recettes anatoliennes traditionnelles revisitées au goût du jour ; vous trouverez également un café typique et une cave.
HISTOIRE	L'hôtel a ouvert ses portes en 2004.
LES « PLUS »	La plage privée est à 4 km.

A Personal Paradise
Atami Hotel, Bodrum

Atami Hotel, Bodrum

A Personal Paradise

When Atakan from Turkey and Midori from Japan fell in love with one another, he was a young engineer and she a stewardess who flew around the world on board Lufthansa aircraft. Together they landed in Istanbul, where Atakan ran a sticky-tape factory, and spent long years in the metropolis. Their dream, however, was always a house by the sea – for themselves and their friends, in the midst of unspoilt nature and far away from any neighbour, a flower-filled garden and a coast with crystal-clear water on the doorstep. Atakan travelled up and down the Turkish coast in search of the perfect spot – until he struck it lucky on the peninsula of Bodrum, and at the secluded Cennet Koyu ("Paradise Bay") laid the foundation stone for the Atami Hotel. Today, the family welcomes here those who wish to experience surroundings that have remained wonderfully unchanged while enjoying hikes or water sports (the hotel's floating marina is just marvellous!) and who are curious to find out about a special mix of cultures. From her Asian homeland, Midori has brought Yoga to Turkey; in her Ikebana courses she shows how filigree Japanese flower arrangements are created, and she spoils her guests with the finest sushi – here she charmingly insists that orders arrive an hour in advance, so that the raw fish can be prepared completely fresh. It is best to enjoy it on the panoramic terrace, which, like all the well-tended rooms, looks out onto the Cennet Koyu – Atakan and Midori's personal paradise.

Book to pack: "Mémed, My Hawk" by Yaşar Kemal.

Atami Hotel
Cennet Koyu Cad. No. 48
Gölköy, Bodrum 48400
Turkey
Tel. +90 252 3577 416 and +90 252 3577 417
Fax +90 252 3577 421
info@atamihotel.com and
reservations@atamihotel.com
www.atamihotel.com
Open all year round

DIRECTIONS	Located directly on the beach of Paradise Bay, 2 miles from Gölköy and 25 miles from Bodrum Airport.
RATES	€
ROOMS	10 deluxe and 19 standard rooms, 2 suites.
FOOD	Along with Japanese cuisine, delicious Turkish specialities are served in the "Atami" restaurant.
HISTORY	The Öztaylan family began construction in the early 1990s and carried out almost all of it themselves. The hotel was opened in 2005.
X-FACTOR	The pool high above the bay.

Ein persönliches Paradies

Als sich der Türke Atakan und die Japanerin Midori ineinander verliebten, war er ein junger Elektroingenieur und sie eine Stewardess, die an Bord der Lufthansa durch die Welt flog. Gemeinsam landeten sie in Istanbul, wo Atakan eine Klebebandfabrik leitete, und verbrachten lange Jahre in der Metropole. Ihr Traum war jedoch immer ein Haus am Meer – für sich selbst und Freunde, inmitten unberührter Natur und weit entfernt vom nächsten Nachbarn gelegen, einen blühenden Garten und eine Küste mit kristallklarem Wasser direkt vor der Tür. Auf der Suche nach dem perfekten Platz reiste Atakan die türkische Küste auf und ab – so lange, bis er auf der Halbinsel von Bodrum fündig wurde: An der einsamen Cennet Koyu (»Paradiesbucht«) legte er den Grundstein zum Hotel Atami. Hier empfängt die Familie heute alle, die eine wunderbar ursprünglich gebliebene Umgebung beim Wandern oder Wassersport erleben möchten (die schwimmende Marina des Hotels ist einfach herrlich!) und neugierig auf eine besondere Mischung der Kulturen sind. Midori hat aus ihrer asiatischen Heimat Yoga in die Türkei mitgebracht, sie zeigt in Ikebana-Kursen, wie die filigranen japanischen Blumenarrangements entstehen und verwöhnt ihre Gäste mit feinstem Sushi – hier besteht sie charmant auf einer Stunde Vorbestellungszeit, damit der rohe Fisch ganz frisch zubereitet werden kann. Am besten genießt man ihn auf der Panoramaterrasse, die wie alle der gepflegten Zimmer direkt auf die Cennet Koyu blickt – das persönliche Paradies von Atakan und Midori.

Buchtipps: »Mémed mein Falke« von Yaşar Kemal und Kurzgeschichten von Cevat Şakir Kabaağaçlı (auf Deutsch liegen zum Beispiel vor: »Reise in die Ferne« und »Dschura«).

Un paradis à soi

Quand Atakan le Turc et Midori la Japonaise tombèrent amoureux l'un de l'autre, il était un jeune électrotechnicien et elle, une hôtesse de l'air de la Lufthansa qui parcourait le monde. Ensemble, ils atterrirent à Istanbul où Atakan était directeur d'une usine de ruban adhésif et passèrent de longues années dans la métropole. Ils rêvaient de posséder une maison au bord de la mer, pour eux et leurs amis, au milieu d'une nature intacte et loin de tout voisinage, avec un jardin fleuri et une côte aux eaux cristallines au pied de leur porte. En quête de l'emplacement idéal, Atakan parcourut toute la côte turque jusqu'à ce qu'il trouve ce qu'il cherchait sur la péninsule de Bodrum. C'est dans la baie solitaire de Cennet Koyu (« baie du paradis ») qu'il posa la première pierre de l'hôtel Atami. Aujourd'hui, la famille reçoit tous ceux qui veulent vivre dans un environnement merveilleusement authentique en faisant de la randonnée ou des sports nautiques (la marina flottante de l'hôtel est tout simplement magnifique !) et sont curieux de découvrir un mélange particulier de cultures. Avec le yoga, Midori a introduit le bien-être asiatique en Turquie. Elle montre également pendant des cours d'Ikebana comment faire des compositions florales délicates et régale ses clients des sushis les plus raffinés. A cet effet, elle prie gentiment sa clientèle de bien vouloir passer commande une heure à l'avance pour que le poisson cru soit de première fraîcheur. Consommez-le de préférence sur la terrasse panoramique qui donne, comme toutes les chambres, sur la Cennet Koyu, le paradis personnel d'Atakan et Midori.

Livre à emporter : « Mémed le Faucon » de Yaşar Kemal.

ANREISE	Direkt am Strand der Paradiesbucht gelegen, 3 km von Gölköy und 40 km vom Flughafen Bodrum entfernt.
PREISE	€
ZIMMER	10 Deluxe- und 19 Standardzimmer, 2 Suiten.
KÜCHE	Im Restaurant »Atami« werden neben japanischer Küche auch leckere türkische Spezialitäten serviert.
GESCHICHTE	Die Familie Öztaylan begann Anfang der 1990er mit dem Bau und erledigte fast alle Arbeiten selbst. Eröffnet wurde das Hotel 2005.
X-FAKTOR	Der Pool hoch über der Bucht.

ACCÈS	Au bord de la mer dans une baie paradisiaque, à 3 km de Gölköy et à 40 km de l'aéroport de Bodrum.
PRIX	€
CHAMBRES	10 chambres Deluxe et 19 standard, 2 suites.
RESTAURATION	Au restaurant « Atami », outre la cuisine japonaise, sont servies aussi de délicieuses spécialités turques.
HISTOIRE	La famille Öztaylan a commencé les travaux au début des années 1990 et a presque tout entrepris elle-même. L'hôtel a ouvert ses portes en 2005.
LES « PLUS »	La piscine au-dessus de la baie.

Between Orient and Occident
Hôtel Nord-Pinus Tanger, Tangier, Strait of Gibraltar

Hôtel Nord-Pinus Tanger, Tangier, Strait of Gibraltar

Between Orient and Occident

When the French woman Anne Igou discovered this former palace of a pasha during a stroll though Tangier's Casbah, it was love at first sight. She bought the riad just a few days later and transformed it into a hotel that both gives the impression of a treasure chest and acts as a mirror of the cosmopolitan ambience and the exotic Bohemian world of Tangier. Thanks to its international reputation, in the 20th century the White City on Morocco's northern coast, once shaped by Romans, Byzantines and Arabs, and then later by the Portuguese, Spanish and British, attracted creative minds from both Europe and the United States. This is where Delacroix and Matisse drew, Duke Ellington and Dizzy Gillespie played, Paul Bowles and Tennessee Williams wrote. All of them would surely have felt comfortable in the Nord-Pinus, and they would have continually had to choose a new favourite from the five guest rooms, because Anne Igou constantly changes the interior, combining antique bronze beds with modern butterfly chairs, Moroccan "zellige" tiles with silk from Rajasthan and colourful Middle Eastern glass windows with black-and-white photographs by Peter Lindbergh. To prevent this eclectic mix of styles getting a little too much, there are terraces covering an area of 2150 square feet: they offer an unhindered view into the wide blue yonder – the sky, the Atlantic and the Mediterranean, which merge together on the horizon.

Books to pack: "The Sheltering Sky" by Paul Bowles and "For Bread Alone" by Mohamed Choukri.

Hôtel Nord-Pinus Tanger
11 Rue du Ryad Sultan Kasbah
Tangier
Morocco
Tel. +212 61 228 140
Fax +212 39 336 363
info@nord-pinus-tanger.com
www.hotel-nord-pinus-tanger.com
Open all year round

DIRECTIONS	Situated at the highest point of the old town, some 8 miles east of Tangier Airport.
RATES	€€€
ROOMS	1 room, 4 suites.
FOOD	In the Moroccan restaurant the "tajines" and the fish are especially recommendable.
HISTORY	The riad, with a typical patio, dates from the 18th century; the hotel was opened in August 2007.
X-FACTOR	Guests are permitted to use the private beach of a nearby hotel.

Ein Märchen zwischen Orient und Okzident

Es war Liebe auf den ersten Blick, als die Französin Anne Igou bei einem Spaziergang durch die Kasbah von Tanger diesen ehemaligen Palast eines Paschas entdeckte – sie kaufte den Riad nur wenige Tage später und verwandelte ihn in ein Hotel, das zugleich wie eine Schatzkiste und wie ein Spiegel des kosmopolitischen Flairs und der exotischen Bohème von Tanger wirkt. Die weiße Stadt an Marokkos Nordküste, einst geprägt von Römern, Byzantinern und Arabern sowie später von Portugiesen, Spaniern und Briten, zog im 20. Jahrhundert dank ihres internationalen Rufes kreative Köpfe aus Europa und den Staaten an. Hier zeichneten Delacroix und Matisse, hier spielten Duke Ellington und Dizzy Gillespie, hier schrieben Paul Bowles und Tennessee Williams. Sie alle hätten sich im Nord-Pinus wohlgefühlt und unter den fünf Gästezimmern immer wieder einen neuen Lieblingsraum gewählt. Denn Anne Igou verändert das Interieur ständig, kombiniert antike Bronzebetten mit modernen Butterfly Chairs, marokkanische »Zellige«-Fliesen mit Seide aus Rajasthan und orientalisch bunte Glasfenster mit Schwarz-Weiß-Fotografien von Peter Lindbergh. Dafür, dass der eklektische Stilmix die Sinne nicht überfordert, sorgen die insgesamt 200 Quadratmeter großen Terrassen: Sie eröffnen den freien Blick ins Blaue – auf den Himmel, den Atlantik und das Mittelmeer, die am Horizont zusammenfließen.
Buchtipps: »Himmel über der Wüste« von Paul Bowles und »Das nackte Brot« von Mohamed Choukri.

Un conte entre l'Orient et l'Occident

Anne Igou eut le coup de foudre pour cette ancienne demeure d'un pacha lors d'une promenade dans la casbah de Tanger. Elle acheta le riad quelques jours plus tard et le transforma en hôtel. Le Nord-Pinus est une malle au trésor et aussi un miroir qui reflète le cosmopolitisme et la bohème exotique de Tanger. Située sur la côte nord du Maroc, la Ville blanche qui a vu se succéder jadis les Romains, les Byzantins et les Arabes puis, plus tard, les Portugais, les Espagnols et les Anglais, attira au XXe siècle des artistes de toute l'Europe et des Etats-Unis grâce à sa réputation international. Des peintres comme Delacroix et Matisse, des musiciens comme Duke Ellington et Dizzy Gillespie ainsi que des écrivains comme Paul Bowles et Tennessee Williams y séjournaient régulièrement. Tous auraient aimé le Nord-Pinus et n'auraient pas su dire laquelle des cinq chambres ils préféraient. Anne Igou change la décoration intérieure constamment, mariant des lits de bronze anciens avec des chaises Butterfly modernes, des zelliges marocains avec de la soie du Rajasthan et des vitraux colorés orientaux avec des photographies en noir et blanc de Peter Lindbergh. Face à ce mélange éclectique, les terrasses d'une surface de 200 mètres carrés veillent à l'apaisement des sens : elles donnent sur un bleu sans limite, sur le ciel, l'Atlantique et la Méditerranée qui ne font plus qu'un à l'horizon.
Livres à emporter : « Un thé au Sahara » de Paul Bowles et « Le pain nu » de Mohamed Choukri.

ANREISE	Auf dem höchsten Punkt der Altstadt gelegen, 12 km östlich vom Flughafen Tanger gelegen.	ACCÈS	Point culminant de la vieille ville, à 12 km à l'est de l'aéroport de Tanger.
PREISE	€€€	PRIX	€€€
ZIMMER	1 Zimmer, 4 Suiten.	CHAMBRES	1 chambre, 4 suites.
KÜCHE	Im marokkanischen Restaurant sind die Tajine und der Fisch besonders zu empfehlen.	RESTAURATION	Au restaurant marocain, les tajines et poissons sont excellents.
GESCHICHTE	Der Riad mit typischem Patio stammt aus dem 18. Jahrhundert, das Hotel wurde im August 2007 eröffnet.	HISTOIRE	Le riad avec son patio typique date du XVIIIe siècle, l'hôtel a ouvert ses portes en août 2007.
X-FAKTOR	Gäste können den Privatstrand eines nahen Hotels nutzen.	LES « PLUS »	Les clients peuvent utiliser la plage privée de l'hôtel voisin.

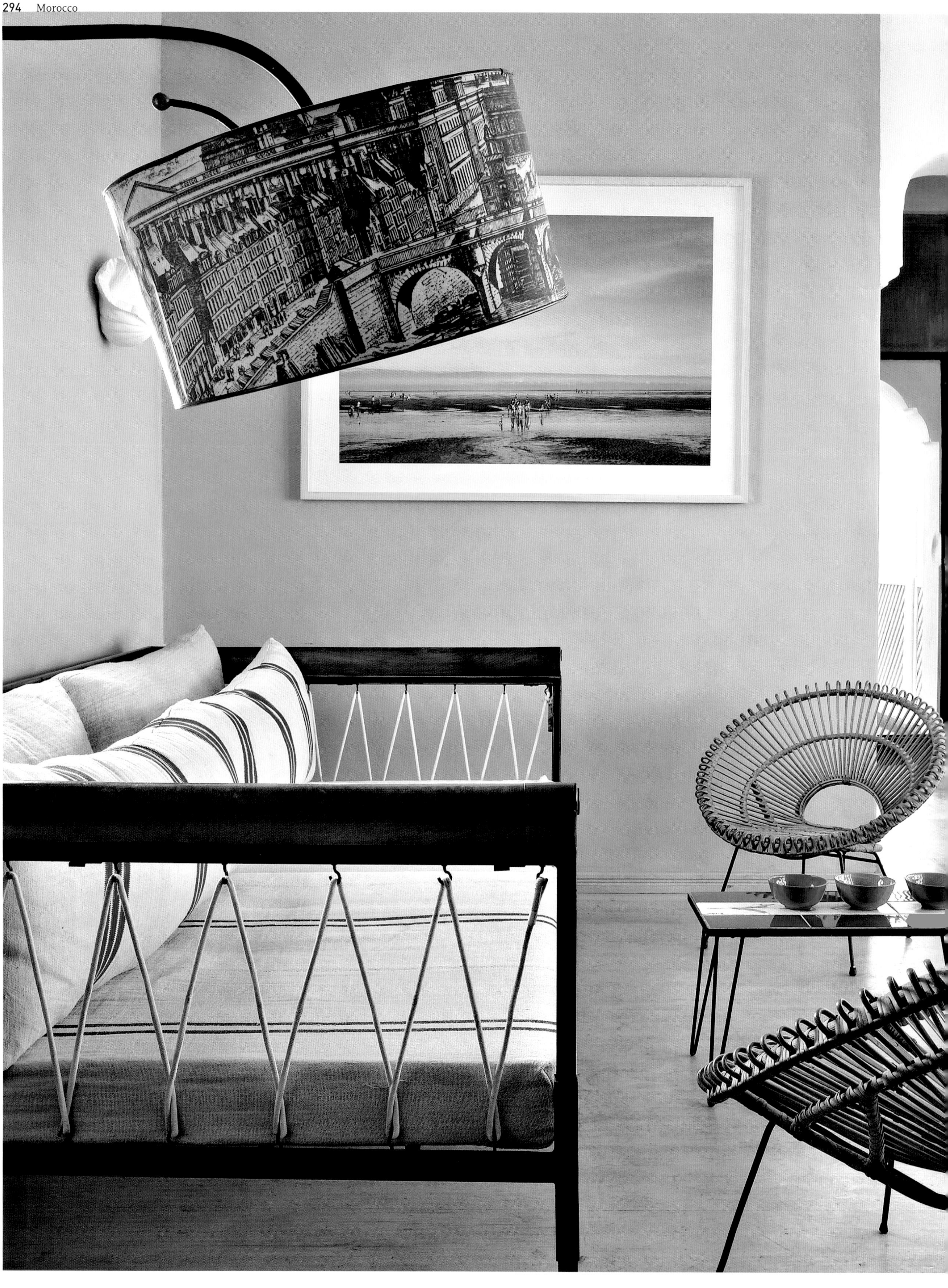

Photo Credits | Fotonachweis
Crédits photographiques

© 2009 TASCHEN GmbH
Hohenzollernring 53, D-50672 Köln
www.taschen.com

To stay informed about upcoming TASCHEN titles, please request our magazine at www.taschen.com/magazine or write to TASCHEN, Hohenzollernring 53, D-50672 Cologne, Germany; contact@taschen.com; Fax: +49-221-254919. We will be happy to send you a free copy of our magazine, which is filled with information about all of our books.

© 2009 FLC/VG Bild-Kunst, Bonn for the works of Le Corbusier.
© 2009 VG Bild-Kunst, Bonn for the works of Harry Bertoia.

COMPILED, EDITED
AND LAYOUT: Angelika Taschen, Berlin
PROJECT MANAGER: Stephanie Paas, Cologne;
                   Nina Schumacher, Cologne
TEXTS: Christiane Reiter, Hamburg
FRENCH TRANSLATION: Cécile Carrion, Cologne
ENGLISH TRANSLATION: Robert Taylor, Cologne
DESIGN: Lambert und Lambert, Düsseldorf
LITHOGRAPH MANAGER: Thomas Grell, Cologne
PRINTED IN   China
ISBN   978-3-8365-1239-8